Logo for Bruno Devos at Stockmans Art Books
designed by Paul Ibou, 2018

Logos on the cover designed by
A   Fernando Medina · Spain
B   Paul Ibou · Belgium
C   MashCreative · United Kingdom
D   Leen Averink · France
E   R. Roger Remington · United States of America
F   DixonBaxi · United Kingdom
G   Robert Geisser · Switzerland
H   Takao Imazu · Japan
I   Jo Vandek · Belgium
J   Boy Bastiaens · The Netherlands
K   Paul Ibou · Belgium
L   KAN · Belgium
M   Yasaburo Kuwayama · Japan
N   Félix Beltrán · Cuba
O   Cato Partners · Australia
P   Paul Ibou · Belgium
Q   DixonBaxi · United Kingdom
R   Bohdan Harbaruk · Ukraine
S   Shreyas Ashok Bendre · India
T   Paul Ibou · Belgium
U   Ramis Guseinov · USSR (Russia)
V   Othmar Motter · Austria
W   Steve Rousso · United States of America
X   Chris Logsdon · United States of America
Y   Burton Kramer · Canada
Z   Studio Meersman · Belgium

Compiled by Christophe De Pelsemaker
www.logo-books.com
www.cedepe.be

© **Concept and cover originally designed by Paul Ibou in 1991**

Printing and production: Bruno Devos / Stockmans, Belgium
www.stockmans.be, www.stockmansartbooks.be

© Stockmans Art Books in collaboration with Logo Books
First published in 2019
ISBN 9789077207642

All rights reserved. No part of this book may be used or reproduced in any matter without prior permission from the copyright holder, except in the context of reviews.

LETTERS AS SYMBOLS
INTERNATIONAL COLLECTION OF LETTERMARKS

Edited and completed by
Christophe De Pelsemaker
in collaboration with Paul Ibou

Christophe De Pelsemaker was born in Anderlecht, Belgium, in 1991. He studied graphic design at Sint-Lukas Brussels and graduated in 2013. De Pelsemaker runs his one-man agency CEDEPE and is the founder of Logo Books, an online book store and publisher specialized in books on logo design. *www.logo-books.com*

Paul Ibou was born in Antwerp, Belgium, in 1939. Ibou graduated from the Royal Academy of Fine Arts in Antwerp (1958) and the Plantin Institute of Typography (1962). In 1962, he started his career as a freelancer based in Antwerp. Ibou received numerous awards and worldwide recognition in specialized press, leading design books and magazines. He was the publisher of more than 50 books on art, design and logo design. In 1994 Ibou organized the first World Symbol Festival in Ostend followed by many others in countries such as China, Korea, Japan, Poland, Mexico, Brazil, Czech Republic,... The festivals were fully devoted to the logo as a symbol represented by and with the presence of leading designers. Today, Ibou is sporadically active as an artist and curator of his personal exhibitions in his own studio.

CONTENTS

FOREWORD — 5
INTRODUCTION — 7
LETTERS AS SYMBOLS — 9

A — 10
B — 20
C — 36
D — 50
E — 60
F — 72
G — 90
H — 106
I — 122
J — 130
K — 136
L — 150
M — 158
N — 172
O — 182
P — 188
Q — 198
R — 206
S — 218
T — 242
U — 256
V — 270
W — 278
X — 288
Y — 296
Z — 304

INDEX — 316
ACKNOWLEDGMENTS — 319
BIBLIOGRAPHY — 320
Featured countries — 320

FOREWORD

Good design is more than a particular style; it is an attitude towards an intrinsic quality. It is why people react against things which are vulgar, fake or unimportant and are drawn to things which have guts, wit and ingenuity. If this sounds more like a moral than an aesthetic attitude, than that is the way how it should be.

When talking about logos, they should neither be linked nor limited to a specific culture but should be understood by people of different cultural backgrounds, worldwide. A logo should be independent of most standards and be accessible to anyone, irrespective of education or level of intelligence. In fact, a logo that is created for a company or organization is intended to ease visual perception. The simpler the form of the logo, the more effectively it catches the human eye.

To maintain its value or prestige, both of which are of vital importance, design must always meet functional and aesthetic requirements based on uniform rules of the principles of design just like language is based on grammar. In recent years these principles have changed very little despite the influence of computers and the cybernetical wave. However, designers have learned quite a lot through experience, including how to conceptualize and simplify. The essence of finding an adequate way of introducing a logo design concept to the public has remained the same. In fact, creating logos and corporate identities still rank among the most rewarding and challenging activities in the field of creativity. Graphic designers are among the most influential visual architects of a better world.

Paul Ibou

INTRODUCTION

Paul Ibou is a man who has done a tremendous amount of work and projects during his career. He belongs to the greatest of all time.

Although he had a strong focus on corporate design and books, these were not his sole occupations. Ibou likes to call himself a multi-artist, which he truly is. He has created numerous paintings and sculptures and he was the founder and president of ITC, International Trademark Center. With ITC, Ibou aimed to group the most important logo designers, exhibit and publish their work. In 1994, this resulted in the World Symbol Festival of which the first edition took place in Ostend. Later, the festival was organized in several other countries worldwide.
The World Symbol Festival was fully devoted to the logo as a symbol, represented by designers who influenced the industry as we know it today. Besides organizing several events himself, Ibou was also member of multiple international juries, accompanied by leaders of the industry of that time.

Ibou was, and still is, an active man in his field and continues carrying fire and passion for constructivist art and graphic design. I was lucky to meet him and receive the opportunity to collaborate with him on this project, Letters As Symbols, which was one of the ideas he still had but never realized.

Since Paul had the idea of Letters As Symbols when he was still in the middle of his career, the original idea was to create a showcase of work from the leading designers of his time. However, the outcome of this project has slightly changed with the intention to add an extra element of surprise and discovery.

The logos featured in Letters As Symbols are a combination of work made by the greatest of all time and of work by contemporary known and unknown designers or agencies. Looking purely at the aesthetics of these logos, they are all equal and have the qualities a good logo must have. Because Paul and I did not want to make a distinction between famous and non-famous designers, the logos are arranged in a non-specific way. The only order that is used is the alphabetical order per letter. This gives you the possibility of being surprised to see the same level of quality between some of the respected leaders and the less known designers.

Christophe De Pelsemaker

LETTERS AS SYMBOLS
INTERNATIONAL COLLECTION OF LETTERMARKS

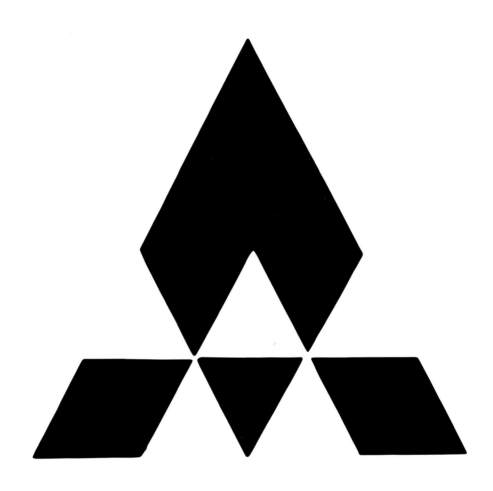

ARTEPIK · CULTURAL CENTER
1970 · Paul Ibou · Belgium

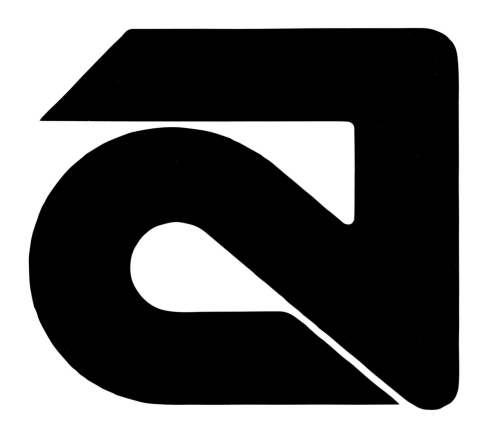

ANGLO-CANADIAN PULP & PAPER · PAPER MANUFACTURING
1973 · Burton Kramer · Canada

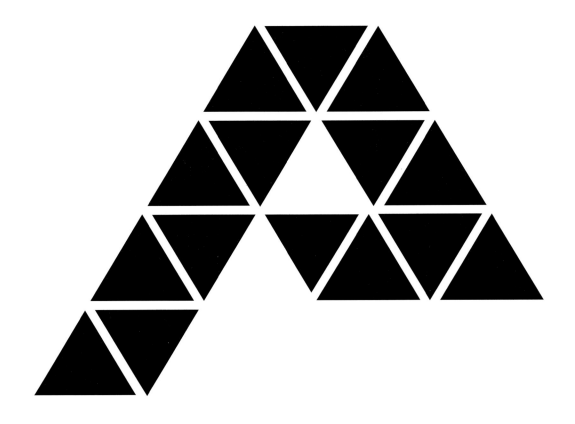

GOVERNMENT OF ANTWERP
1983 · Paul Ibou · Belgium

SOCIÉTÉ FRANÇAISE D'AUTOROUTES · ASSOCIATION OF HIGHWAYS
1975 · Adrian Frutiger · Switzerland

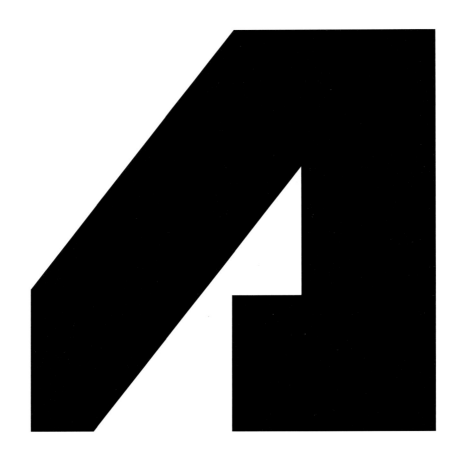

ANDIAMAND
1984 · Erik De Meyer · Belgium

ARTISTAS PLASTICOS ASSOCIATION · ARTIST ASSOCIATION
1979 · Fernando Medina · Spain

AEROTYPE LITHO · PRINTING
1970 · Burton Kramer · Canada

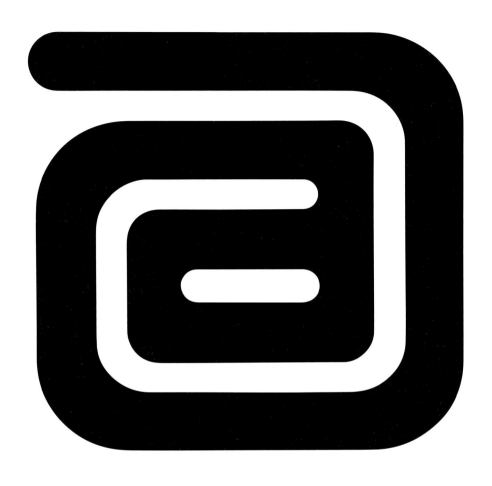

MECHANIKAI MÜVEK · HEATING TECHNOLOGY
1970 · István Szekeres · Hungary

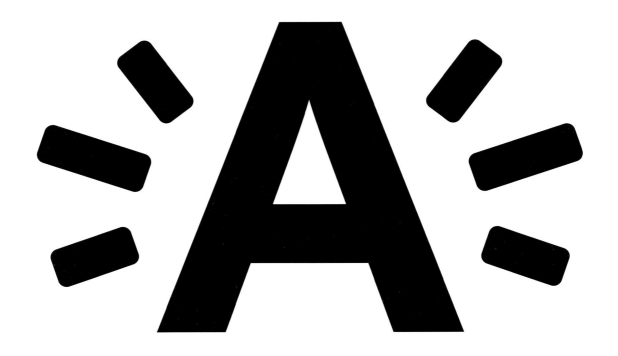

STAD ANTWERPEN · CITY
2004 · LDV United, Redstar Design, Tom Andries · Belgium

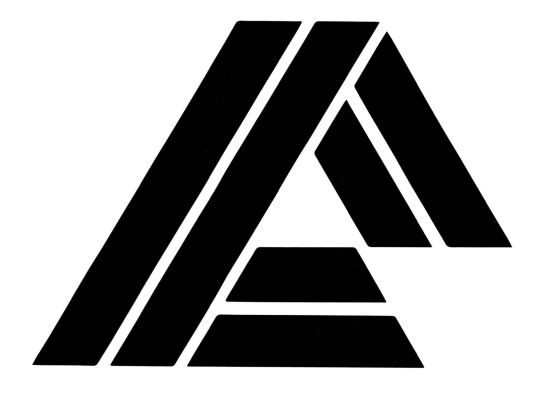

ASTRO PLAN · ROAD CONSTRUCTION
1988 · Francis De Pauw · Belgium

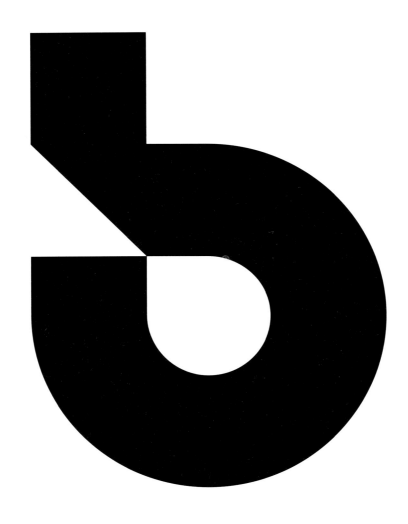

BACKBONE FILMS · FILM PRODUCTION
2018 · Duane Dalton · Ireland

BEAULIEU INTERNATIONAL GROUP · INDUSTRY
2012 · Today · Belgium

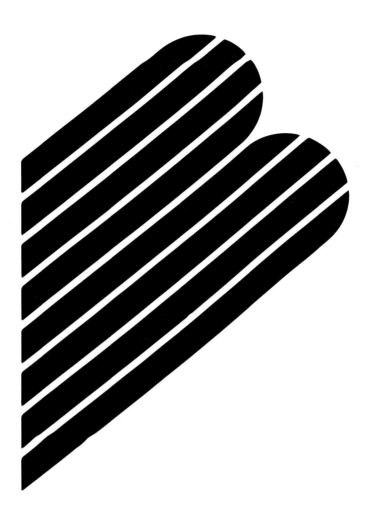

BIBLIOTECA BENJAMÍN FRANKLIN · LIBRARY
1986 · Félix Beltrán · Cuba

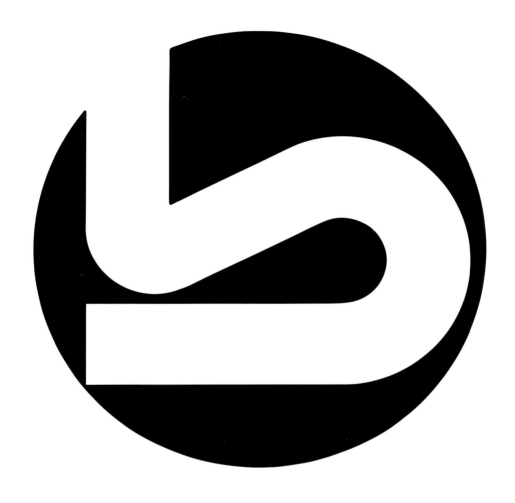

BIENNIAL OF SCULPTURE MIDDELHEIM · ART FESTIVAL
1965 · Paul Ibou · Belgium

BRUGSE BOEKHANDEL · BOOKSTORE
1981 · Johan Mahieu · Belgium

W.H. BRADY
1978 · W.H. Brady · Belgium

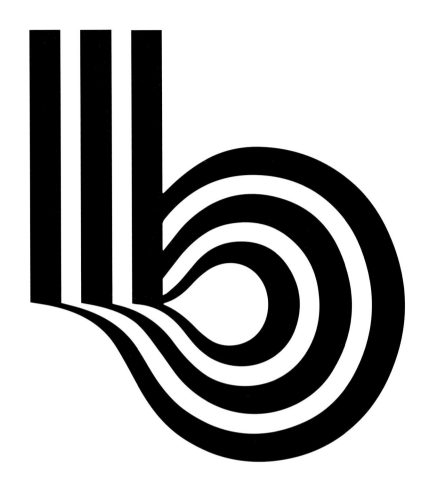

BLOOMING NAKANISHI & COMPANY · TEXTILE
1985 · Shigeo Katsuoka · Japan

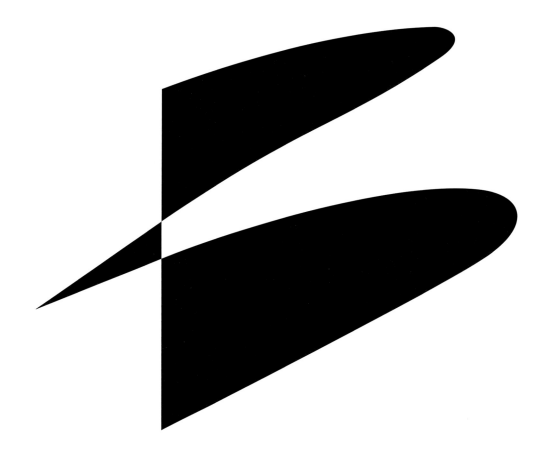

BANESTO · BANK
Félix Beltrán · Cuba

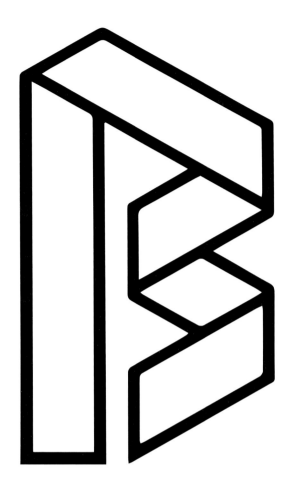

BATEAU LAVOIR · ART GALLERY
1970 · Michele Spera · Italy

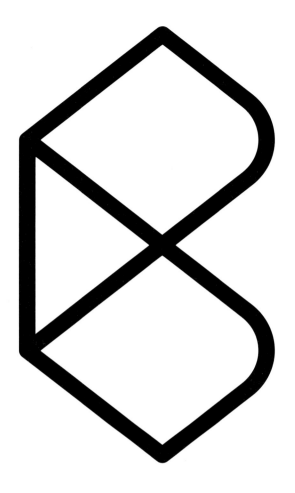

BROOKS SOLUTIONS · CONSTRUCTION
2015 · Jonathan Lawrence · United States of America

R.W. BUELOW ARCHITECTS · ARCHITECT
1981 · Gale William Ikola · United States of America

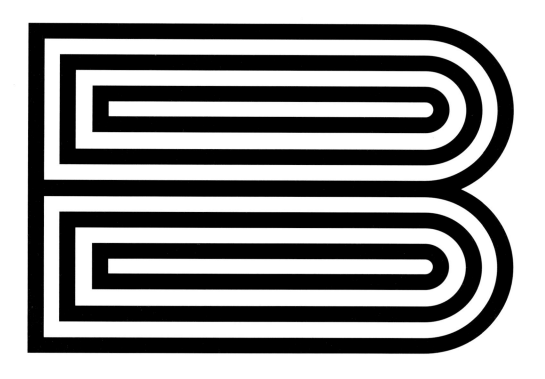

BRNO BIENNIAL · EVENT
1964 · Jiří Hadlač · Czech Republic

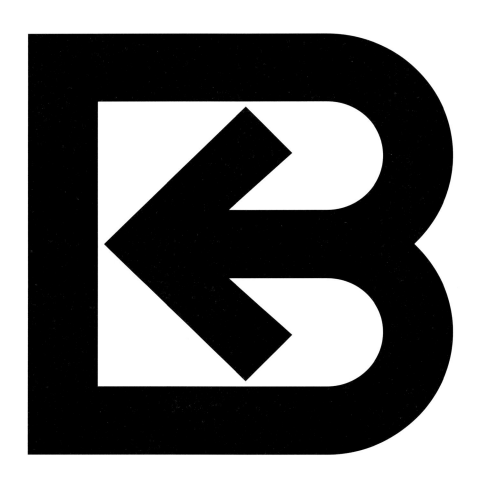

REGINALD BENNETT · IMPORT
1967 · Stuart Ash · Canada

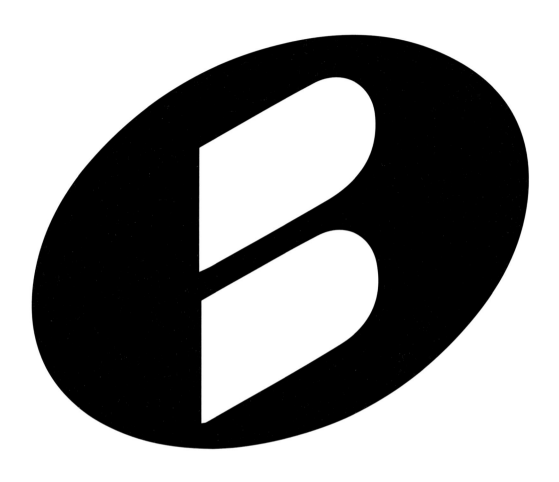

BELLFEED · TEXTILE INDUSTRY
1980 · Akira Hirata, Yoshiharu Saito · Japan

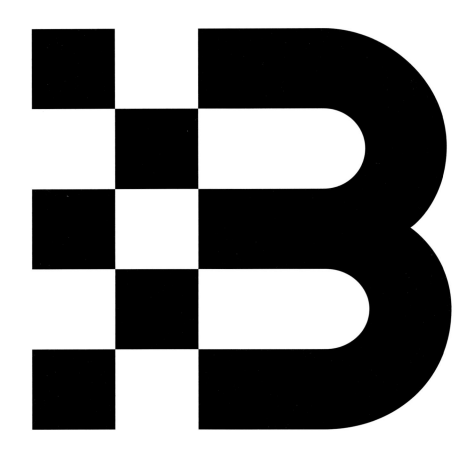

MAX · COSMETICS
1981 · Fumio Koyoda · Japan

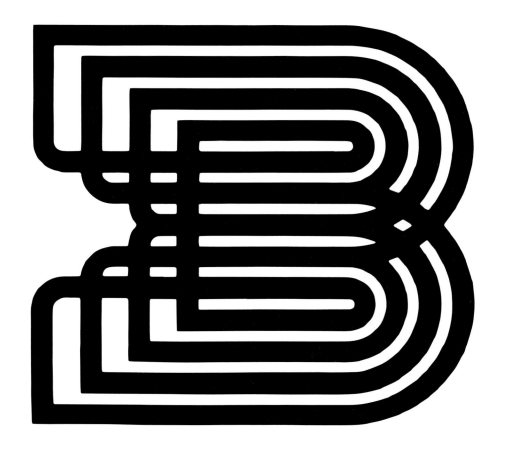

BEDFORD CONSULTING GROUP
1978 · Burton Kramer · Canada

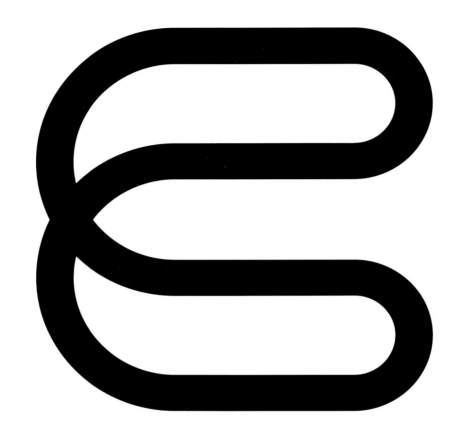

CUSP · KITCHEN APPLIANCES
2014 · MashCreative · United Kingdom

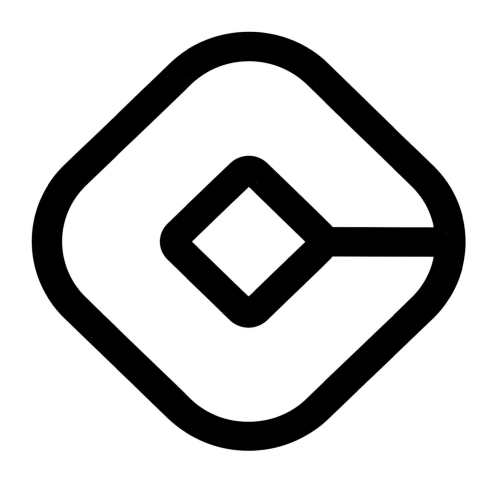

COMPOINT · COMPUTERS
1983 · Jan Van Craesbeeck · Belgium

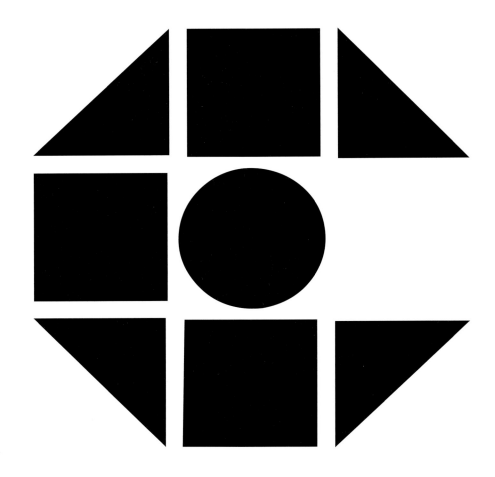

CASSOCHROME · PRINTING
1985 · Paul Ibou · Belgium

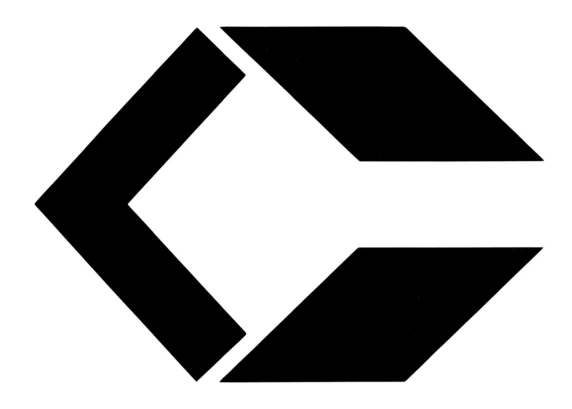

CHARLIER · IMPORT & EXPORT
1965 · Paul Ibou · Belgium

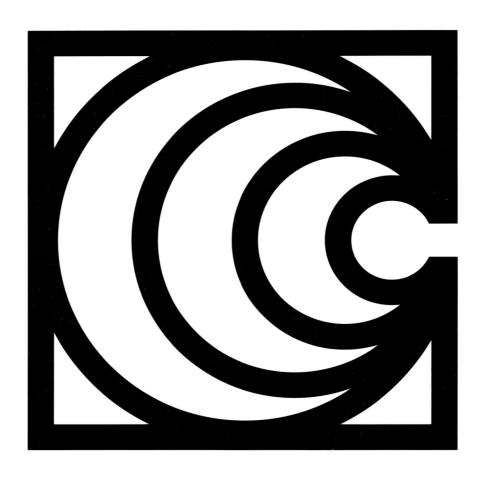

CHROMOSCOPE PICTURES · MOVIE/FILM PRODUCTION
2018 · Chris Logsdon · United States of America

CULTUREEL CENTRUM HEUSDEN · CULTURAL CENTER
Francis Dirix · Belgium

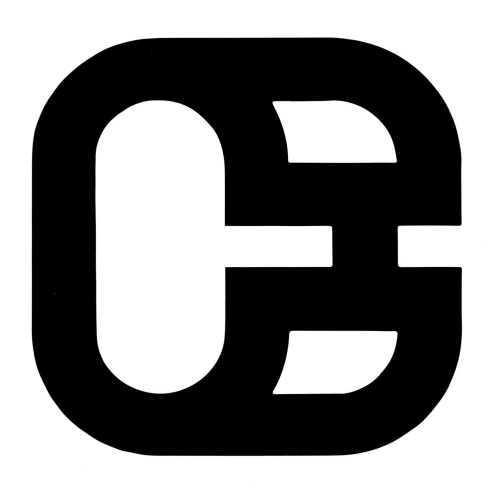

COURANT
1989 · Ravan · Belgium

CREATEX · TEXTILE
1983 · Roger Vansevenant · Belgium

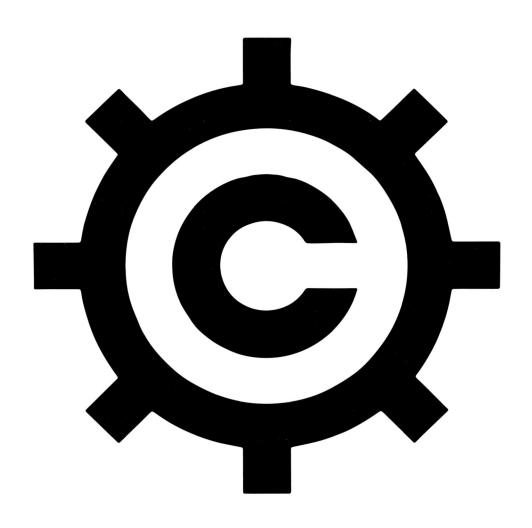

COMEXAS · SHIPPING
1987 · Paul Ibou · Belgium

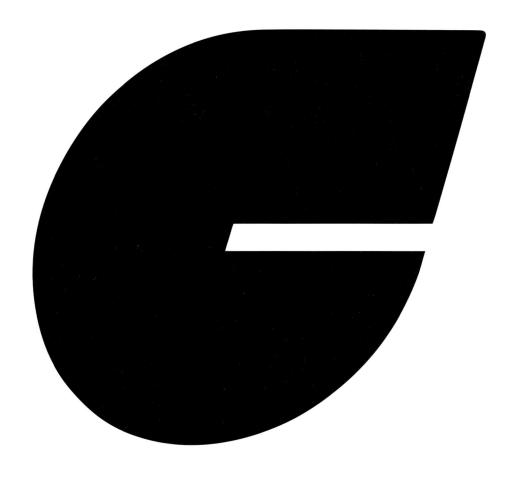

COMMERCE BANK · BANK
1973 · Richard Yeager · United States of America

BANCO COMERCIAL PORTUGUES · BANK
Timing, Alliance · Portugal

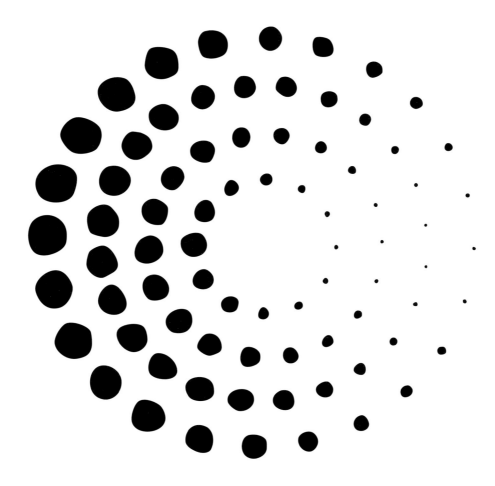

CORALBA · FOOD & DRINKS
2010 · Today · Belgium

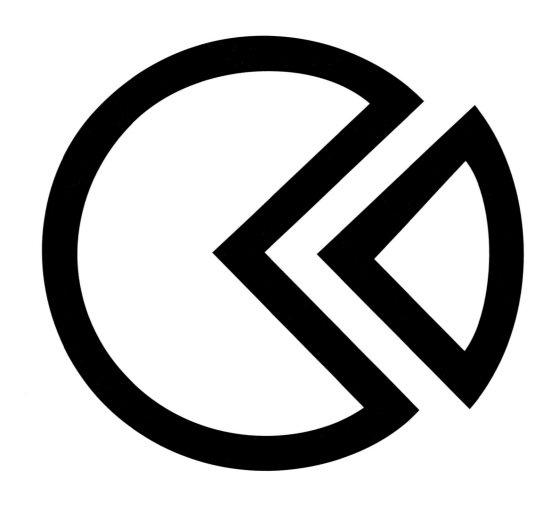

COMPARTIR · EDUCATION
1980 · Dicken Castro · Colombia

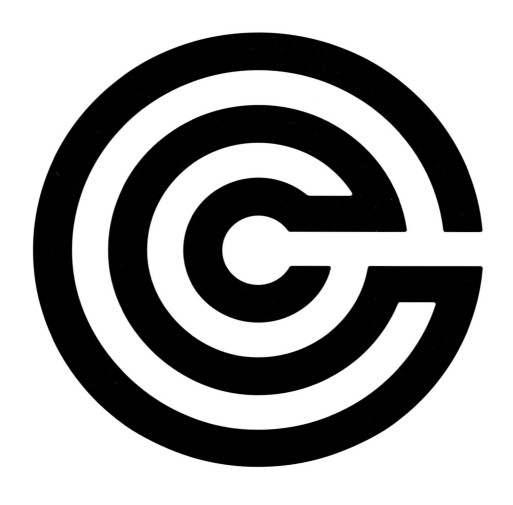

KULTURMARKT DILLINGEN · CULTURE MARKET
1980 · Dieter Urban · Germany

DAVID'S · JEWELRY
1989 · Steve Rousso · United States of America

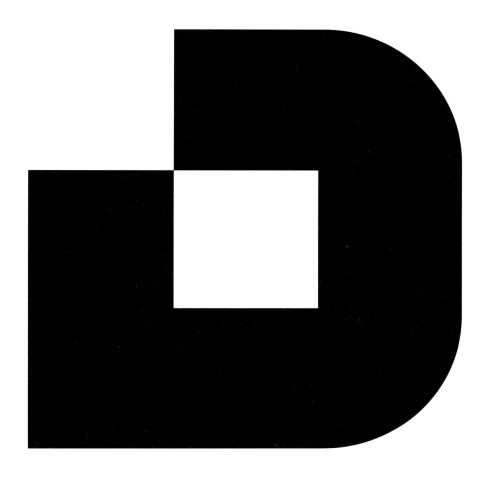

INTERNATIONAL DESIGN & WOODCRAFT · DESIGN
1978 · Rolf Harder · Canada

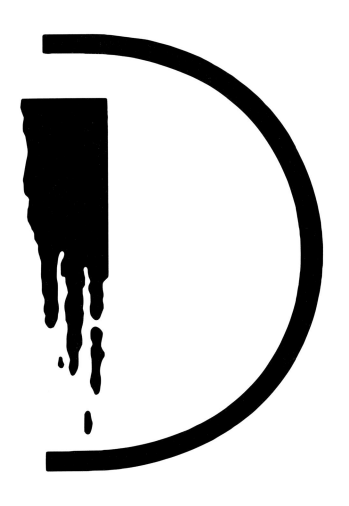

DYANSEN GALLERY · ART GALLERY
1989 · Douglas Doolittle · Japan

DUKANE CORPORATION · COMMUNICATIONS SYSTEMS DIVISION
1975 · William H. Goldsmith · United States of America

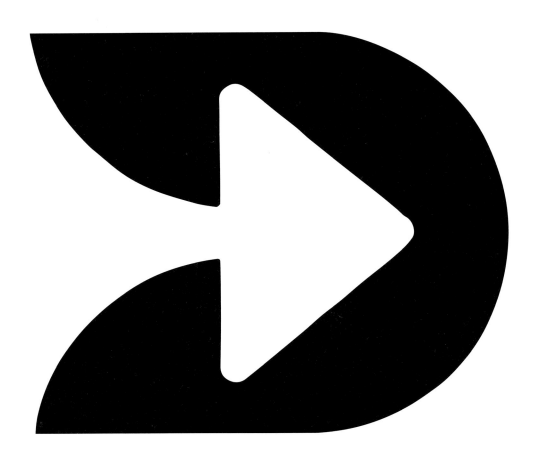

DENOTRA · CONSTRUCTION MATERIALS
1978 · Roger Vansevenant · Belgium

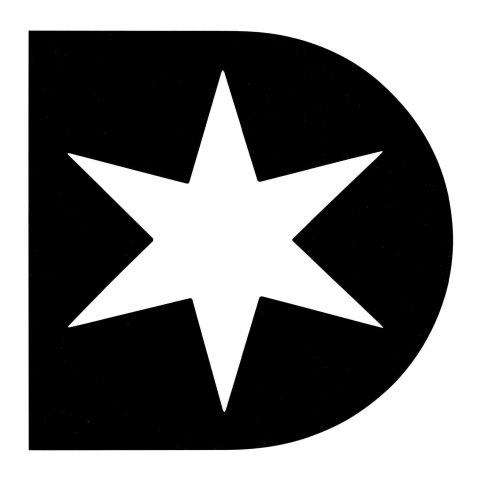

FOTO DEBANDT · PHOTOGRAPHY
1989 · Paul Ibou · Belgium

DE KEMPENEER · ROAD CONSTRUCTION
1973 · Guy Debrouwer · Belgium

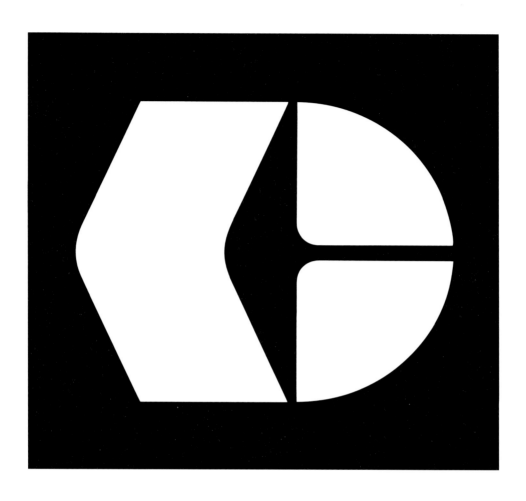

D'HULST · CONSTRUCTION
1974 · Paul Ibou · Belgium

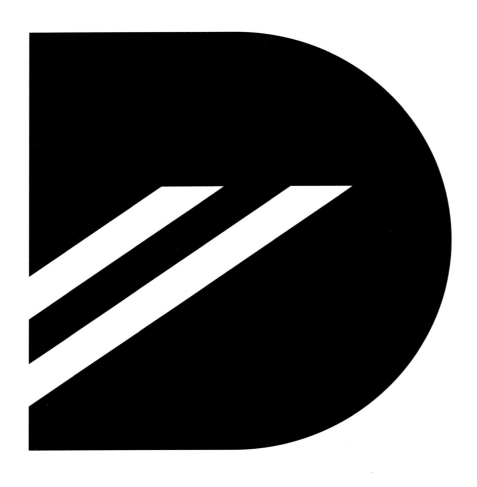

PRZEDSIE BIORSTWO BUDOWY DRÓG I MOSTÓW · ARCHITECT
1976 · Tytus Walczak · Poland

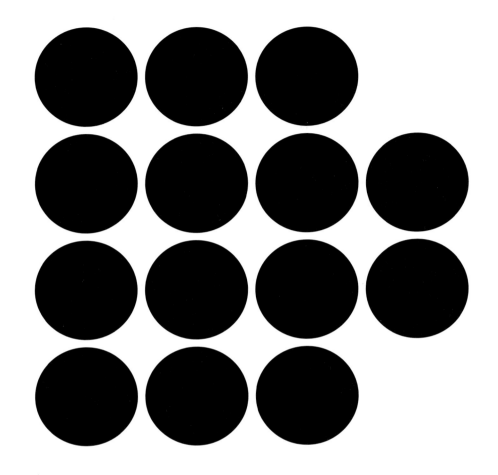

STÉ DAUM · GLASS
1972 · Leen Averink · France

ENTRECANALES Y TAVORA · CONSTRUCTION
1973 · Cruz Novillo · Spain

ANZENKOGAKU KENKYUJO · RESEARCH INSTITUTE
1975 · Shigeo Katsuoka · Japan

DAIICH SEIKO · PLASTIC INDUSTRY
1981 · Ken'ichi Hirose · Japan

ECON TECHNOLOGIES · DIGITAL SYSTEMS INTEGRATION
1975 · R. Roger Remington · United States of America

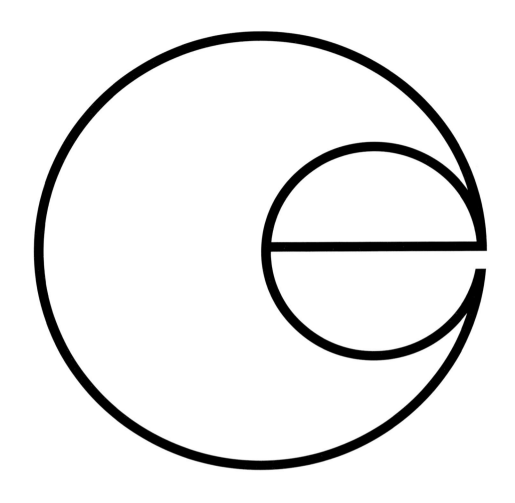

EDITION LEIPZING · PUBLISHING
1975 · Sonja Wunderlich · Germany

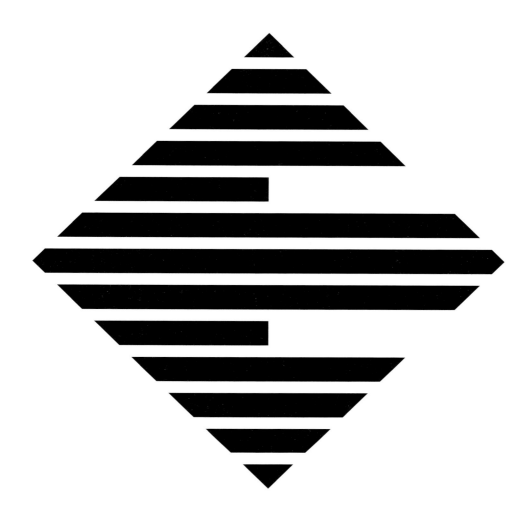

EPACAR · PAPER DISTRIBUTION
1977 · Paul Ibou · Belgium

ELLERMAN COMPANIES INC · INSURANCE
1975 · James Lienhart · United States of America

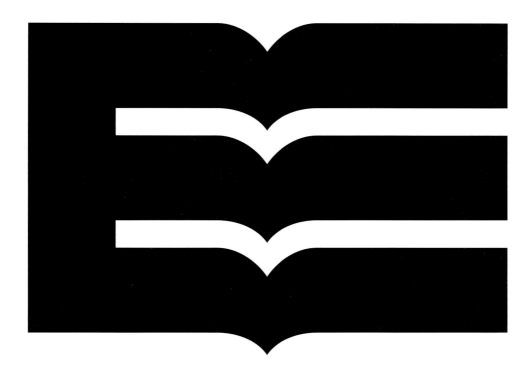

EUROPESE BIBLIOTHEEK BRUSSEL · LIBRARY
1966 · Michel Olyff · Belgium

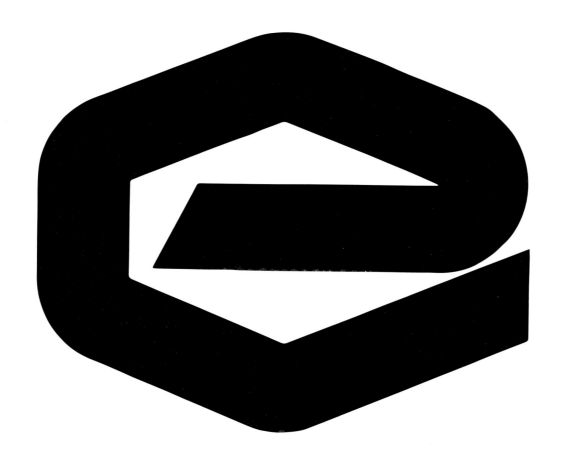

EURIM · ELECTRONICS
1979 · Bernard Vandenbroeke · Belgium

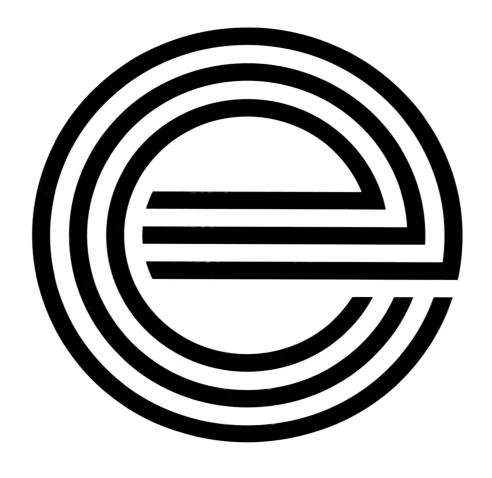

ESSENCE MUSIC · MUSIC PRODUCTION
2015 · Duane Dalton · Ireland

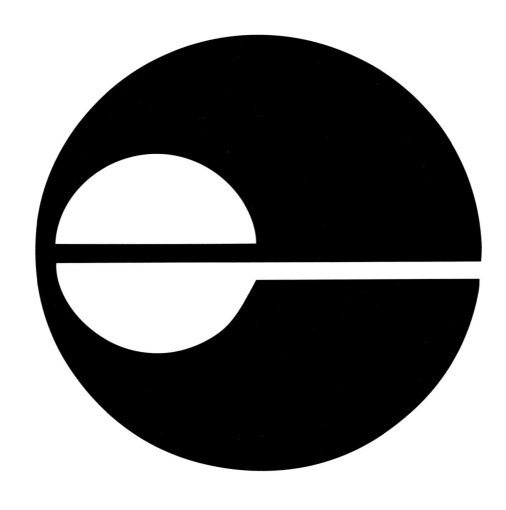

ECODYNAMICS · PRODUCT DEVELOPMENT
1980 · Gerald Gallo · United States of America

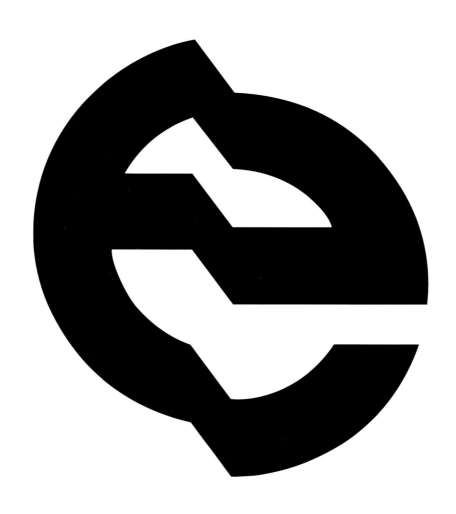

EDILTUR · TRAVEL AGENCY
1975 · Alfredo de Santis · Italy

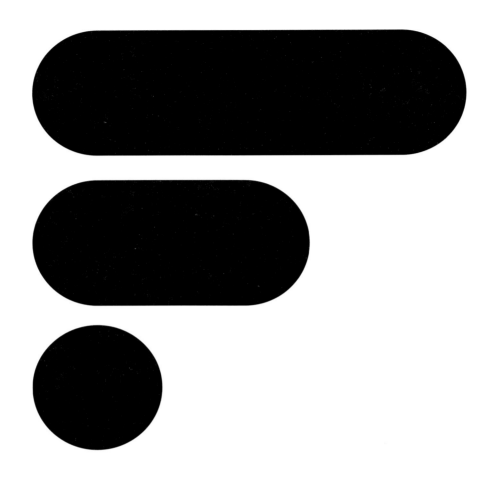

FOODTOWN
Cato Partners · Australia

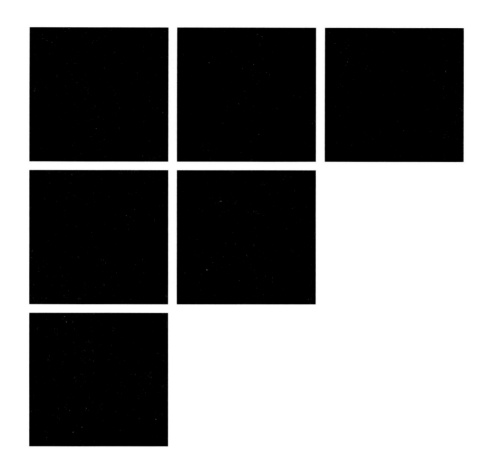

FRISOL · OIL
1981 · Paul Ibou · Belgium

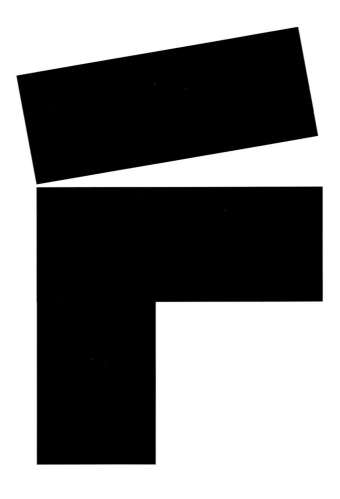

FINE LINE FEATURES · FILM PRODUCTION & DISTRIBUTION
1991 · Woody Pirtle · United States of America

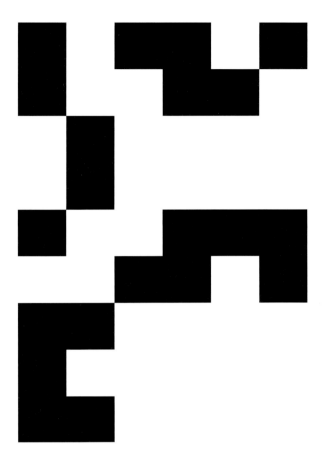

FRUIT MARKET GALLERY · ART GALLERY
1990 · Alan Fletcher · United Kingdom

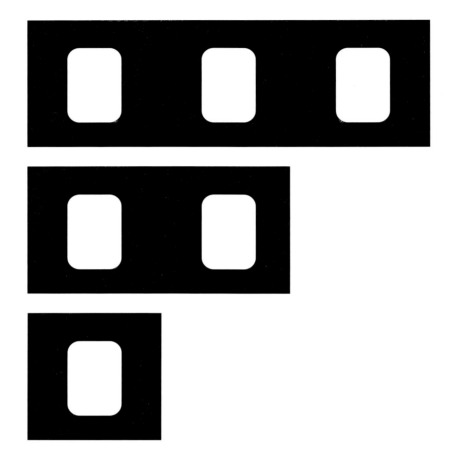

FILM GROUP INTERECHO · FILM PRODUCTIONS
1986 · Paul Ibou · Belgium

FILAD · AFFILIATES ADMINISTRATION
1989 · Filip De Baudringhien · Belgium

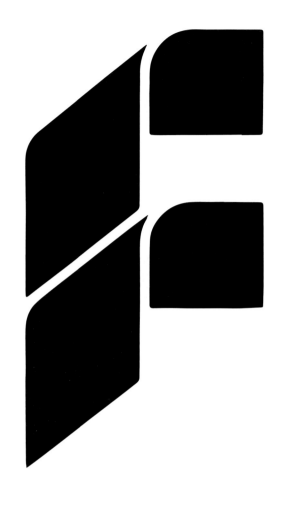

FEBELGRA · GRAPHIC INDUSTRY
1977 · Hayez Drukkers · Belgium

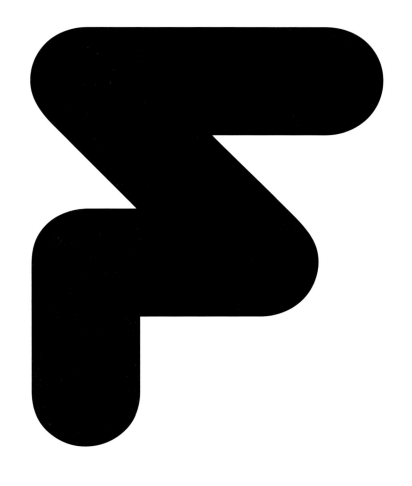

FREEVIEW · MEDIA & TECHNOLOGY
2015 · DixonBaxi · United Kingdom

FURROW BOOKS · PUBLISHING
2013 · Scott Fuller (The Studio Temporary) · United States of America

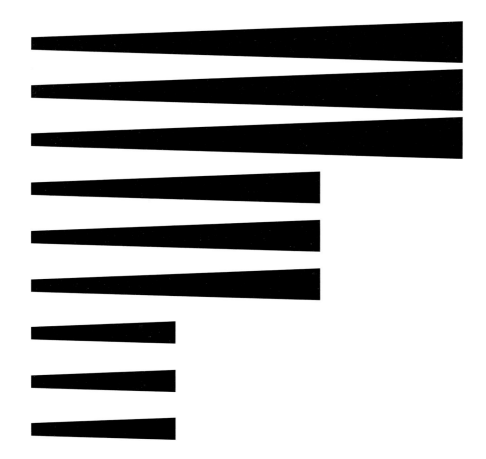

FONDATION DE L'HÔTEL-DIEU · HOTEL
1982 · Frederic Metz · Canada

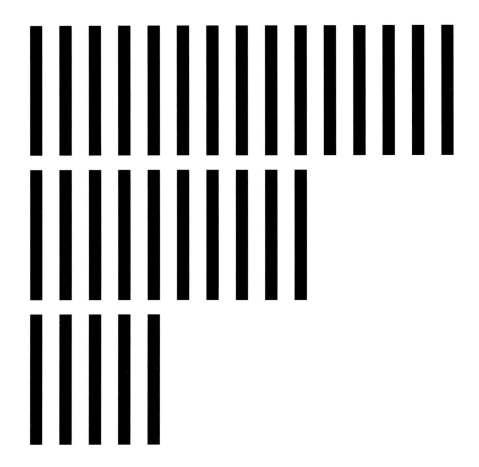

FINAMEX · BANK
Félix Beltrán · Cuba

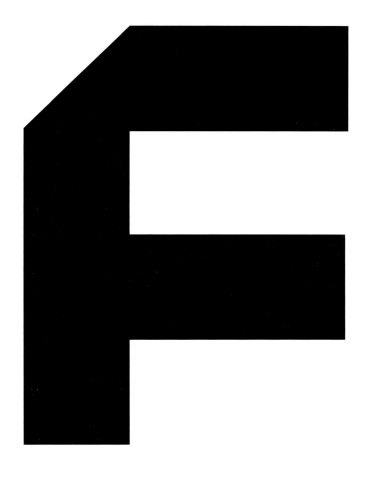

FRIESLAND BANK · BANK
1973 · Wim Crouwel · The Netherlands

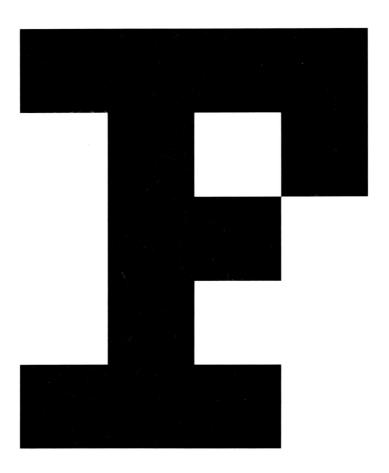

FLAX
1949 · Louis Danziger · United States of America

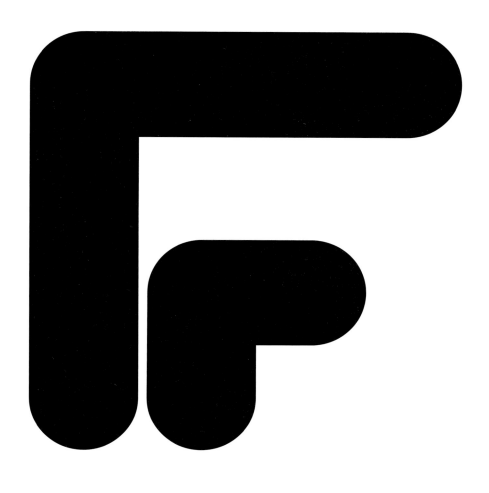

FEDERAL CEI SPA · MACHINERY
1976 · Carlo Malerba · Italy

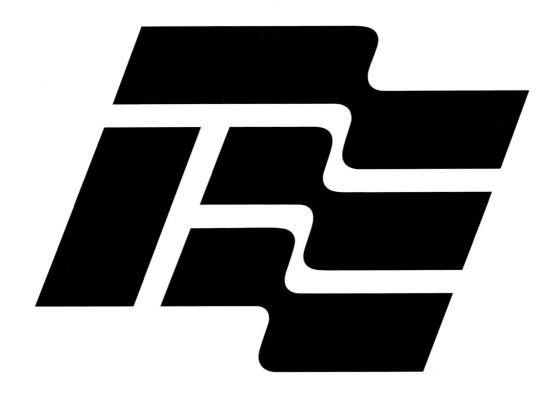

FLAGG INDUSTRIES INC · CONGLOMERATE
1972 · Ray Engle · United States of America

FRIGERIO · TRANSPORT
1983 · A. Ubertazzi, D. Soffientini, R. Nava · Italy

KAZUYA FUKADA · ACCOUNTING
1983 · Toshio Fukano · Japan

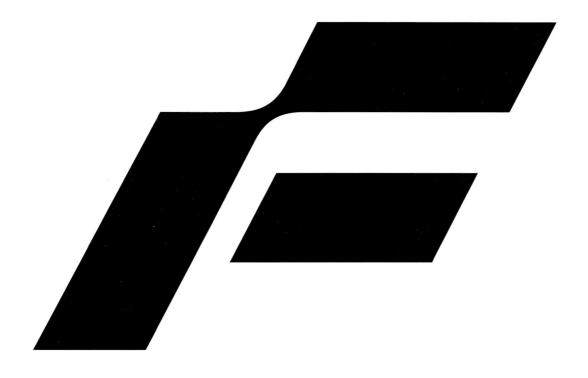

TERASAKI KOGYO · TOBACCO
1982 · Ikuo Masubuchi · Japan

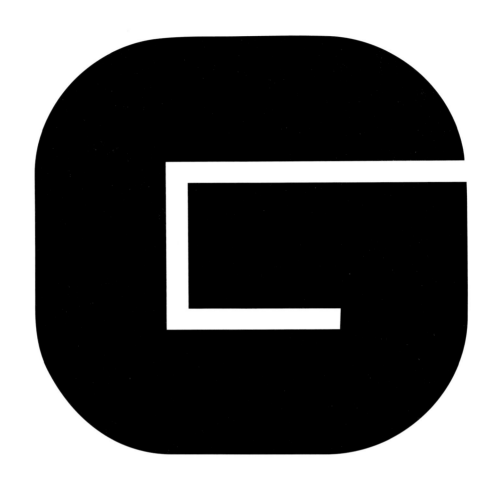

GARY INTERNATIONAL BANK · BANK
1970 · James Lienhart · United States of America

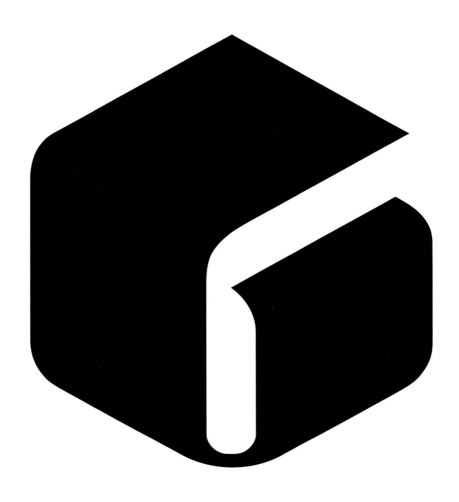

TRUST GÉNÉRAL DU CANADA · BANK
1983 · Réal Séguin · Canada

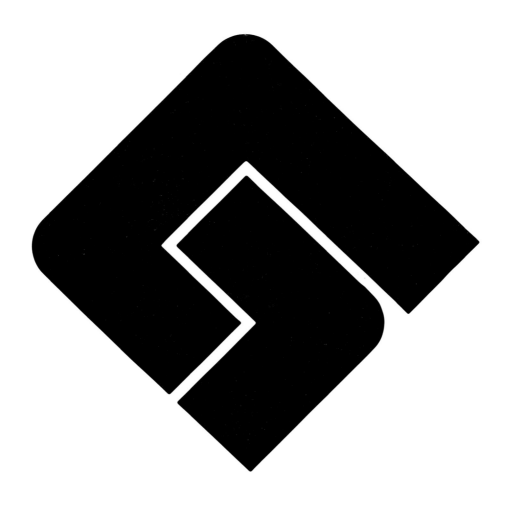

GYPKA · PLASTERBOARDS
1980 · Bernard Vandenbroeke · Belgium

GENERALE BANK · BANK
1968 · Jaques Richez · Belgium

GEELEN · CLOTHING
1973 · Francis Dirix · Belgium

DRUKKERIJ GOVAERTS · PRINTING
1976 · E. De Pelseneer · Belgium

GRAPHIC CONTROLS CORPORATION
1986 · Graphic Controls Corporation · Belgium

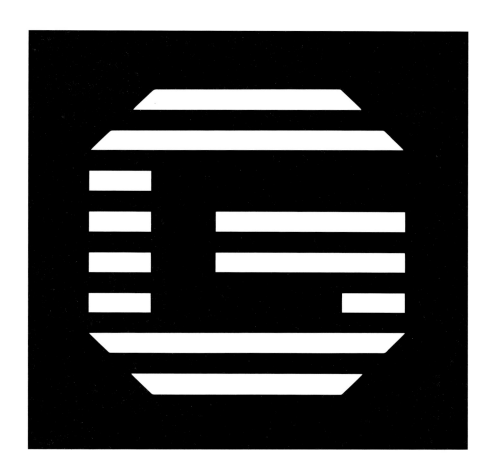

GUMA · FOOTWEAR
1989 · Paul Ibou · Belgium

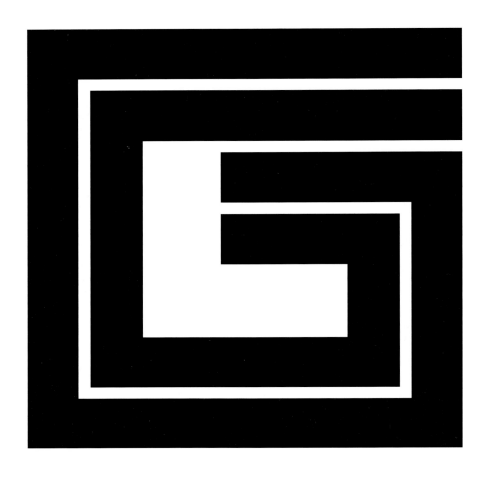

GOYVAERTS GASPARD · ACCOUNTANCY
1971 · Paul Ibou · Belgium

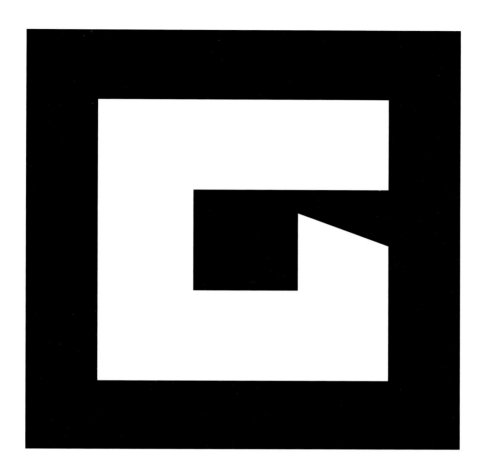

HANS-JOACHIM GERIKE
1966 · Klaus Grözinger, Peter Riefenstahl · Germany

GRAPHIC CENTER · PRINTING
1968 · Robert Geisser· Switzerland

GIRARD BANK · BANK
1960 · Emil O. Biemann · United States of America

GOLDEN GUERNSEY DAIRY · DAIRY PRODUCTION
1975 · Doris Stein · United States of America

GRAPHIC DESIGNERS ASSOCIATION JAPAN · DESIGNERS ASSOCIATION
1979 · Kazuo Kishimoto · Japan

MECHANISCHE WERKSTÄTTE · MECHANICS
1980 · Walter Hergenröther · Germany

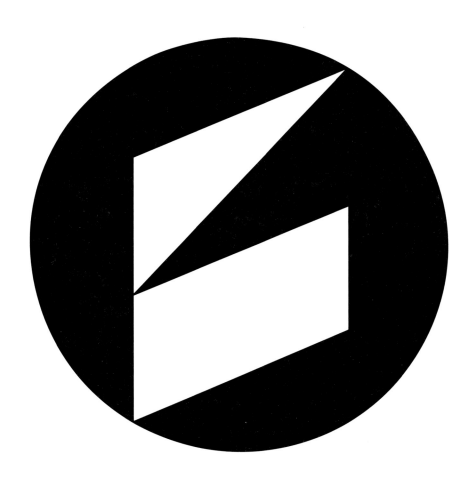

MAIZURU LIQUEFIED GAS · GAS
1985 · Sukeyasu Kannou · Japan

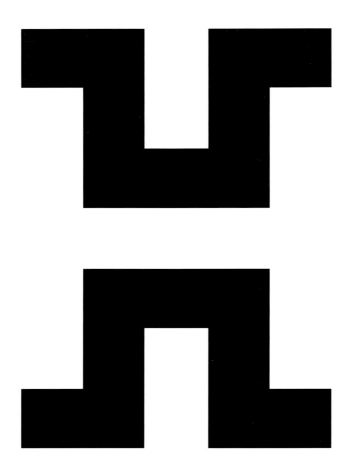

HOTEL HUASTECA · HOTEL
1987 · Félix Beltrán · Cuba

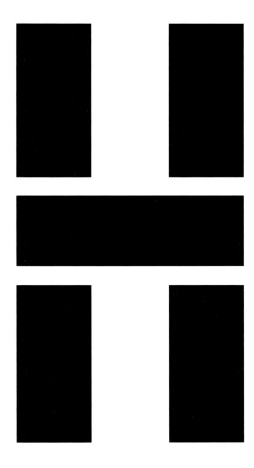

HECHINGER COMPANY · HOME-IMPROVEMENT STORES
1975 · Ivan Chermayeff, Tom Geismar · United States of America

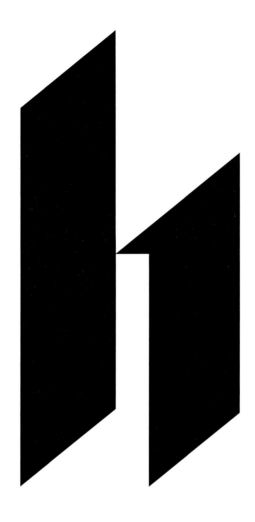

HŌEI KENSETSU · CONSTRUCTION
1984 · Takuo Ōtakara · Japan

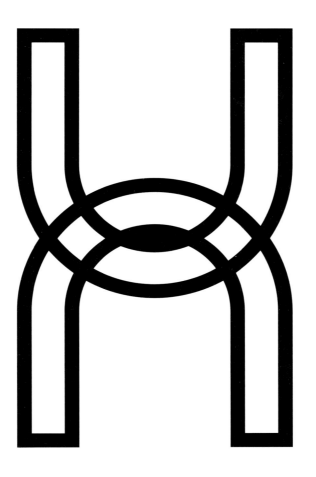

HERA · CLOTHING
1973 · Roger Vansevenant · Belgium

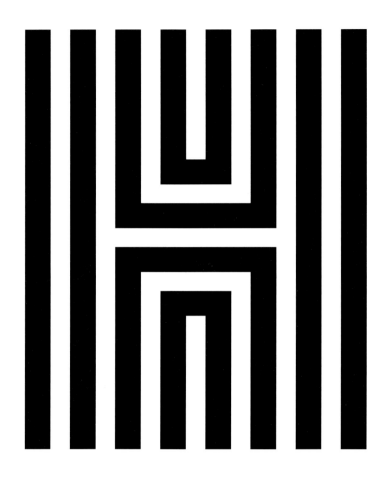

HELON · ACCOUNTANCY
1981 · Rik Annerel · Belgium

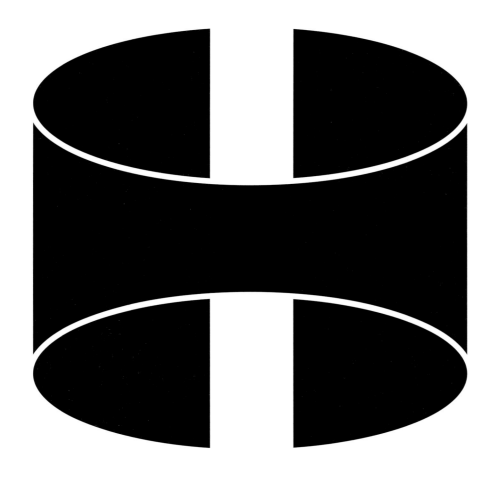

HOUTLAND
1979 · Studio Artex · Belgium

HIGIA · PHARMACEUTIC DISTRIBUTION
1986 · Armando Ferraro Senior · Venezuela

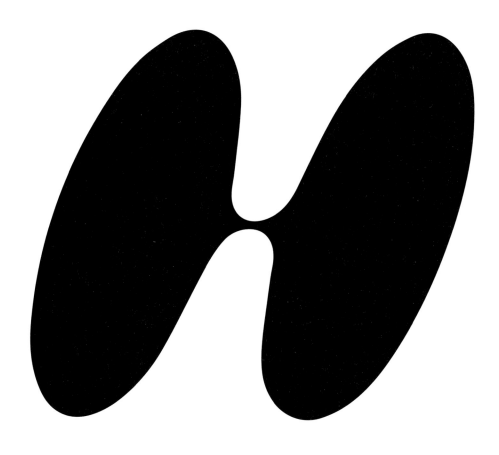

HARVEST · SERVICE INDUSTRY
1987 · Takao Imazu · Japan

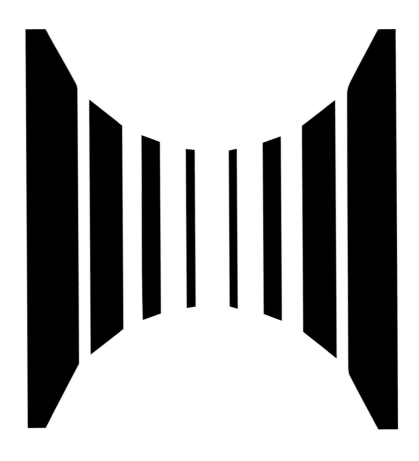

HIBINO CORPORATION · SOUND EQUIPEMENT
1988 · T. D. Narimatsu · United States of America

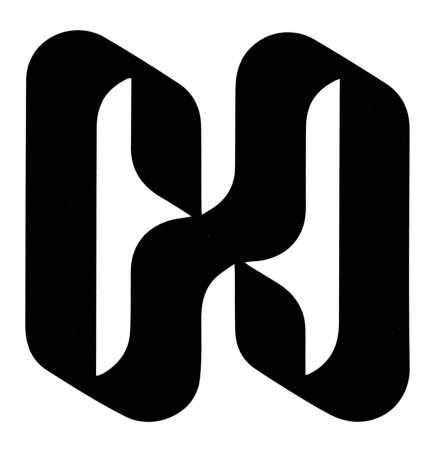

HOKUSHIN · PRINTING
1982 · Soichi Saito · Japan

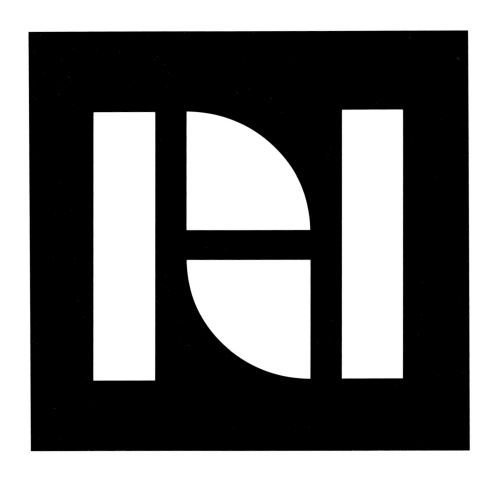

HYDROGEN SYSTEMS · NUCLEAR PRODUCTIONS
1985 · Paul Ibou · Belgium

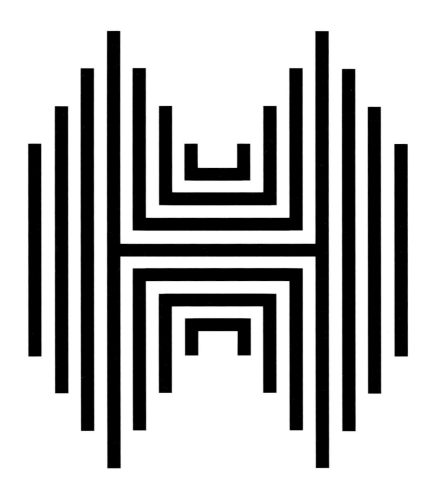

HALKBANK · BANK
Ira Advertising · Turkey

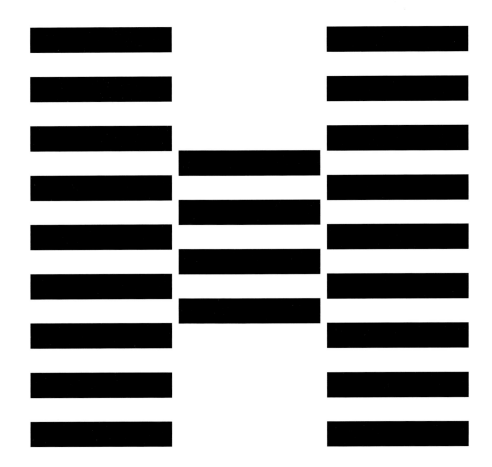

HELIOMEX · TELEVISIONS
1982 · Félix Beltrán · Cuba

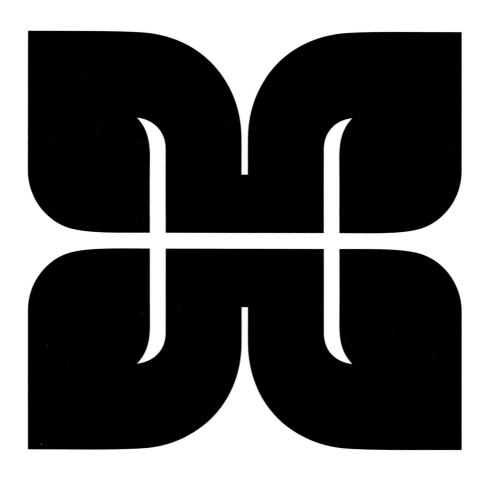

HALLMARK HOTELS · HOTEL
1977 · Burton Kramer · Canada

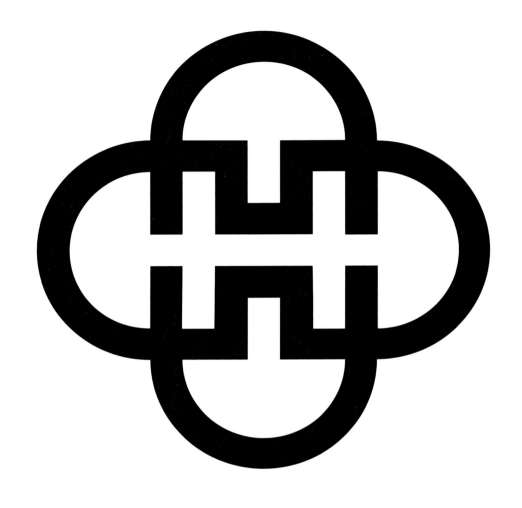

HERITAGE CAMBRIDGE · ARCHITECTURAL CONSERVANCY
1970 · Glenn Fretz · Canada

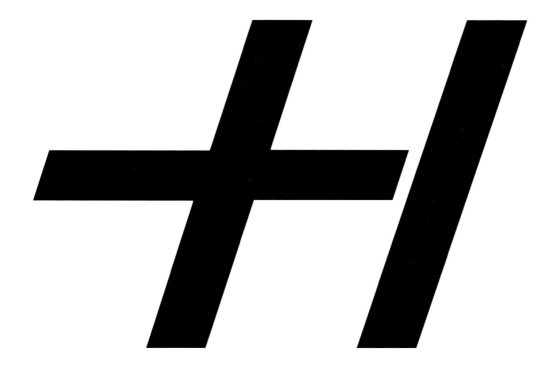

HENO WATCH · WATCHES
1964 · Adrian Frutiger · Switzerland

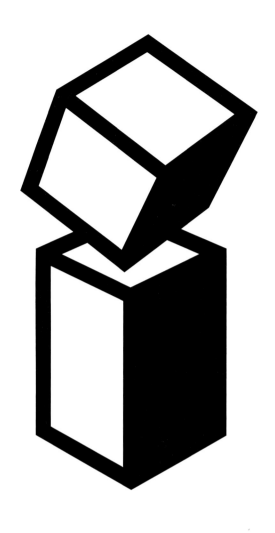

ICHIKEN INC · CONSTRUCTION
1989 · Katsuichi Ito · Japan

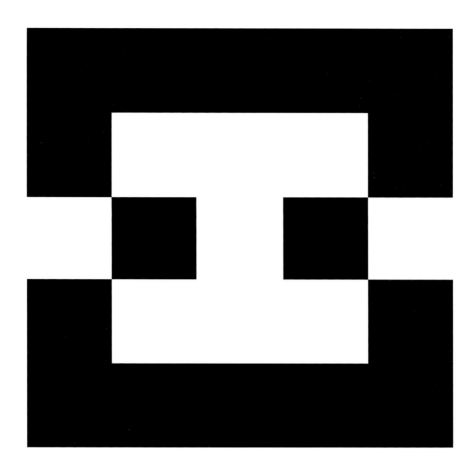

IANUA · CONSTRUCTION
1977 · Guillermo Gonzalez Ruiz · Brazil

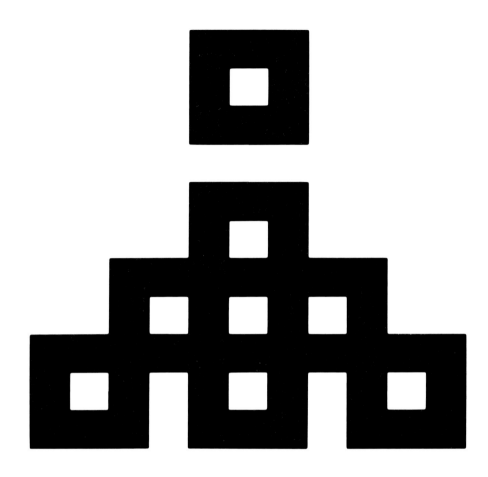

INTERECHO PRESS · PUBLISHING
1985 · Paul Ibou · Belgium

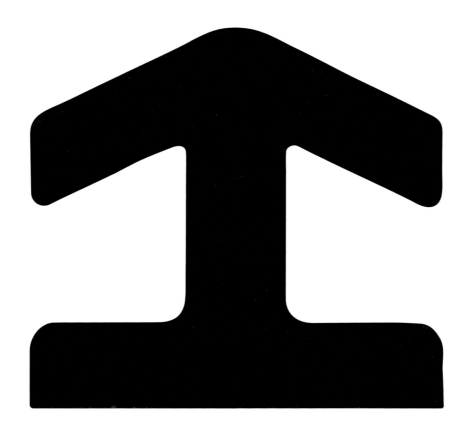

INTERSELEX · INVESTING
1971 · Guy Schockaert · Belgium

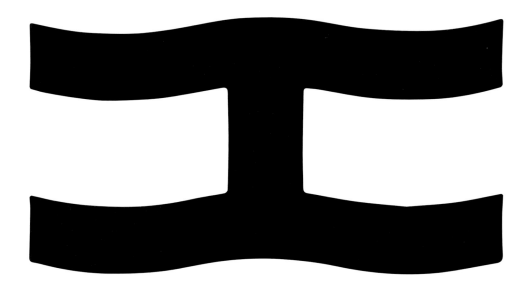

UITGEVERIJ INTER-BOOK · PUBLISHING
1970 · Herbert Binneweg · Belgium

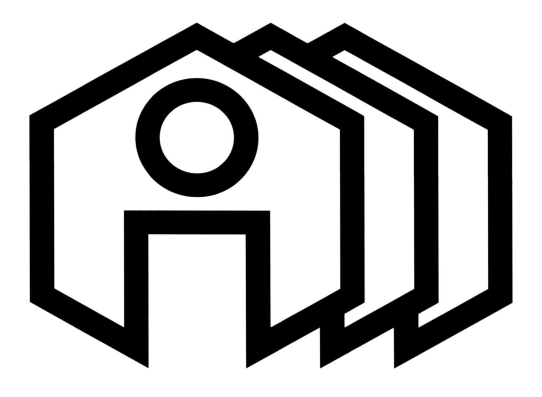

INVESTIMMO · REAL ESTATE
1986 · Paul Ibou · Belgium

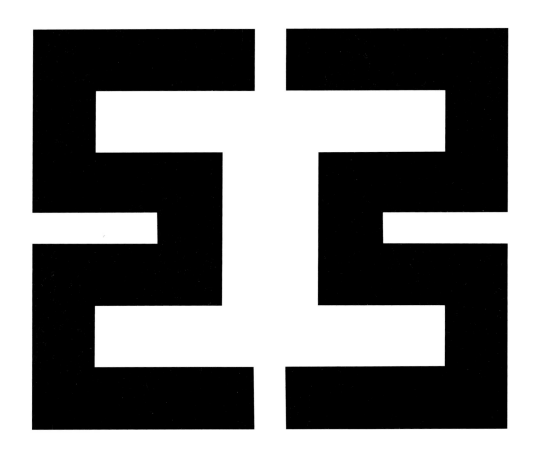

INTERNATIONAL BANK OF ASIA · BANK
Henry Steiner · Austria

INTERSCRIPT
1977 · Jo Vandek · Belgium

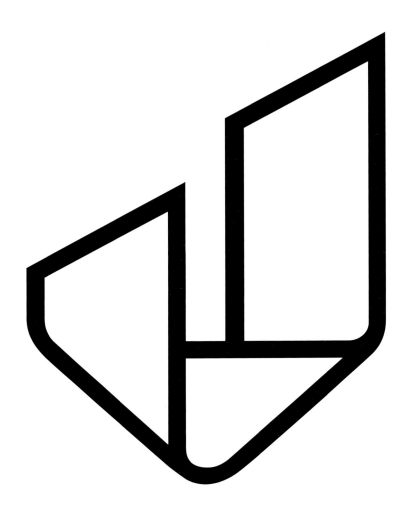

JERTON
1989 · Edi Berk · Slovenia

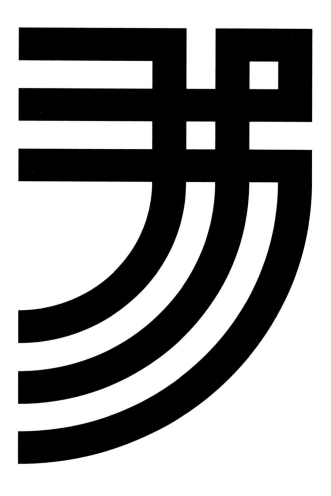

PAUL JAMBERS · TELEVISION CELEBRITY
1994 · Paul Ibou · Belgium

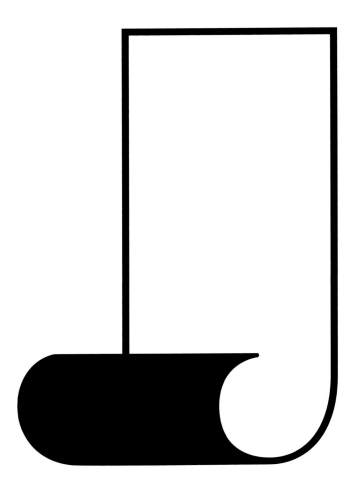

G. JANTSCH'S PRINTING OFFICE · PRINTING
1980 · Hermann Zapf · Germany

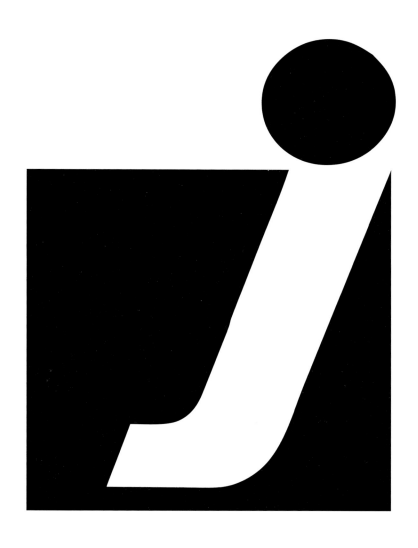

BOMBAY TOOLS SUPPLYING AGENCY · TOOLS
1979 · Ajit S. Chavan, Raju D. Bind · India

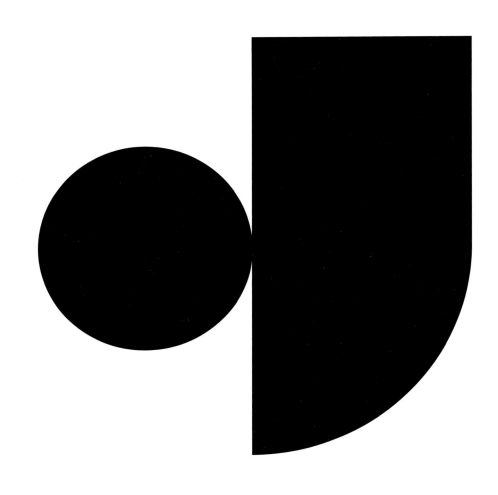

J´HERRENMODE · APPAREL
1968 · Otto Krämer · Switzerland

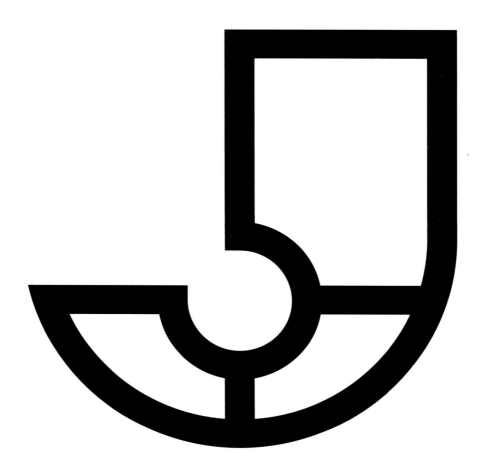

JETTSON · SNEAKERS & SPORTSWEAR
2015 · Boy Bastiaens · The Netherlands

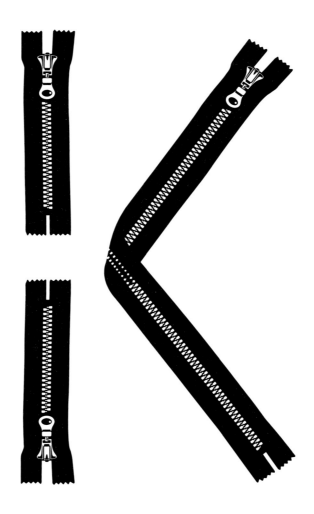

KARL LAGERFELD · FASHION
2008 · Boy Bastiaens · The Netherlands

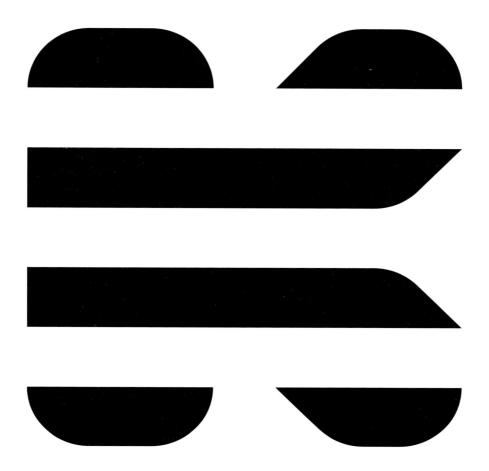

KUBO HEALTH
2017 · Jeroen van Eerden · The Netherlands

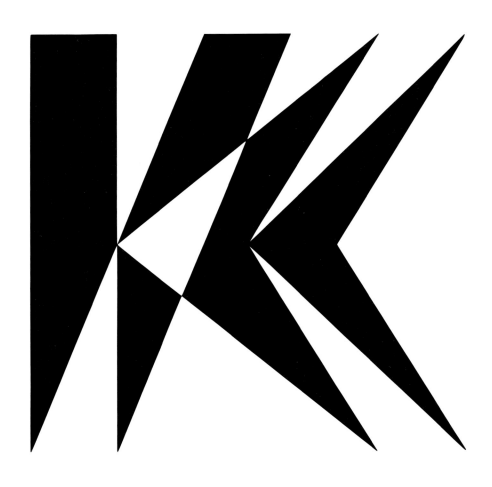

KOMKOMMER · JEWELRY
1978 · Paul Ibou · Belgium

KINGSLEY JEWELRY · JEWELRY
2017 · Jeroen van Eerden · The Netherlands

KOCHI BANK · BANK
Mitsuo Hosokawa · Japan

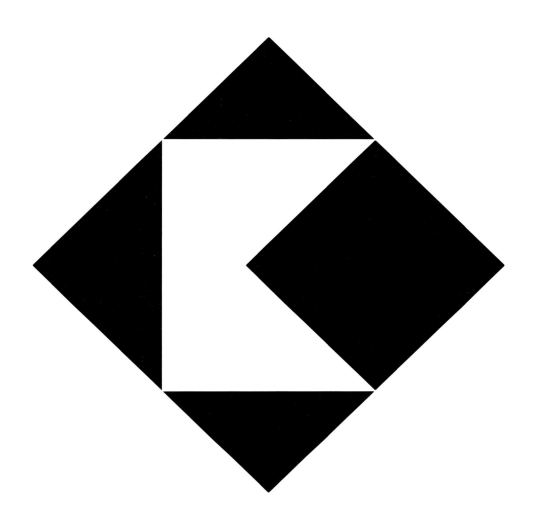

MUSEUM OF ART KATONAH · MUSEUM
Ivan Chermayeff, Tom Geismar · United States of America

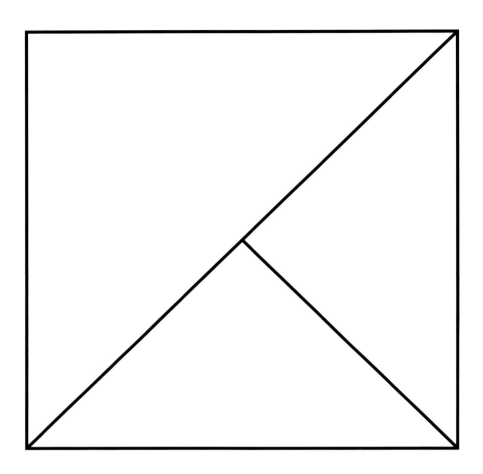

STÄDTISCHE KUNSTHALLE DÜSSELDORF · ART GALLERY
1967 · Walter Breker · Germany

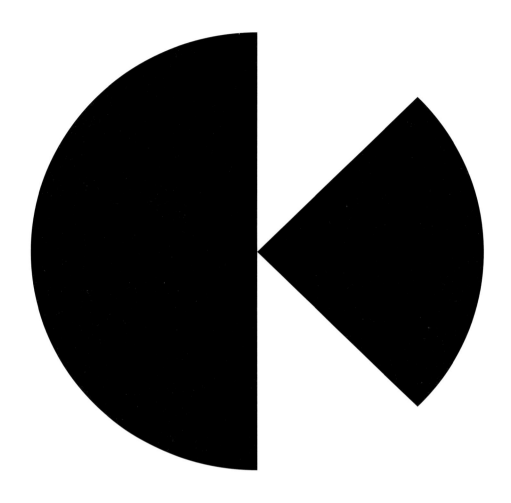

AGENCE KER · ADVERTISING AGENCY
1970 · Jean-Claude Müller · United States of America

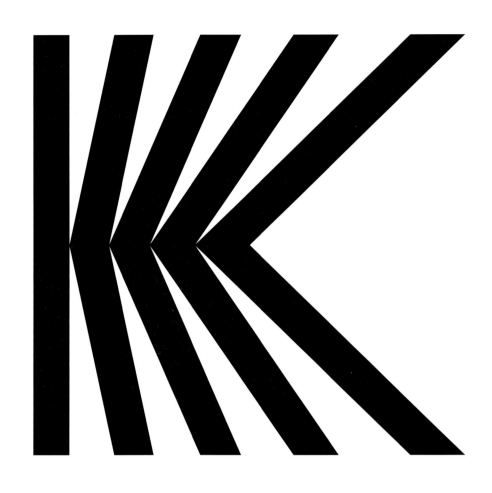

KANBE · TEXTILE
1973 · Akisato Ueda · Japan

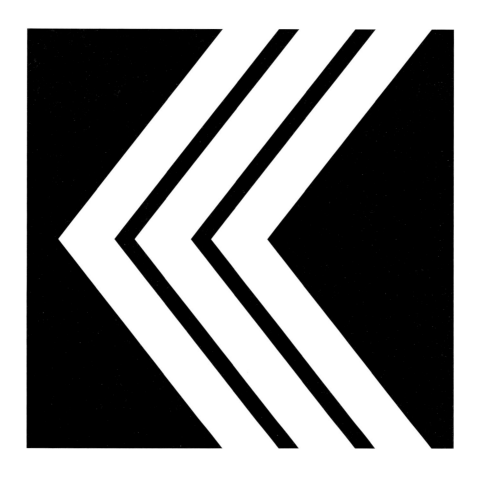

KANEDA ENTERPRISE · TRADING COMPANY
1983 · Hiroshi Toida · Japan

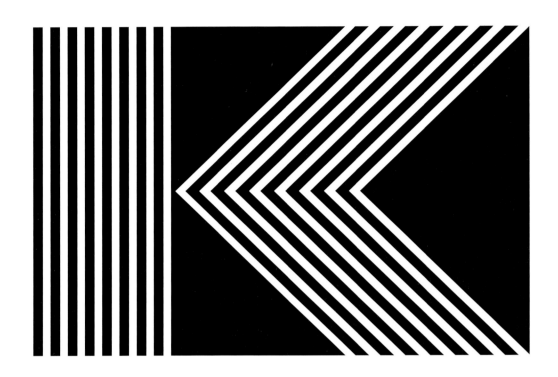

KELLOCK FACTORS · INVESTING & BROKER
1976 · Kenneth Hollick · United Kingdom

KLEIBER · PLASTICS
1981 · Othmar Motter · Austria

KRAMER DESIGN ASSOCIATES LTD
1982 · Burton Kramer · Canada

FOUNDATION OF FINNISH INVENTIONS
1986 · Esko Miettinen · Finland

LENZING AG · CHEMICAL FIBRES
1984 · Friedrich Eisenmenger · Austria

LANNOO · PUBLISHING
1999 · KAN · Belgium

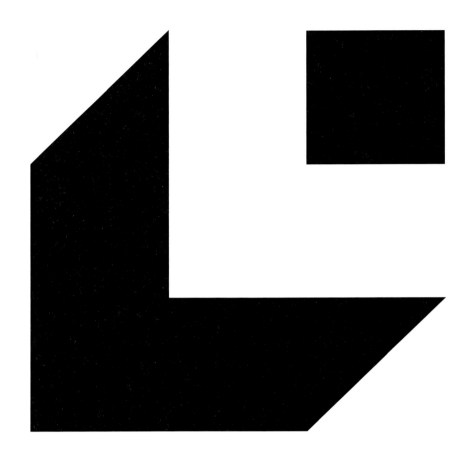

LA LUXEMBOURGEOISE · INSURANCES
Interpub' · Luxembourg

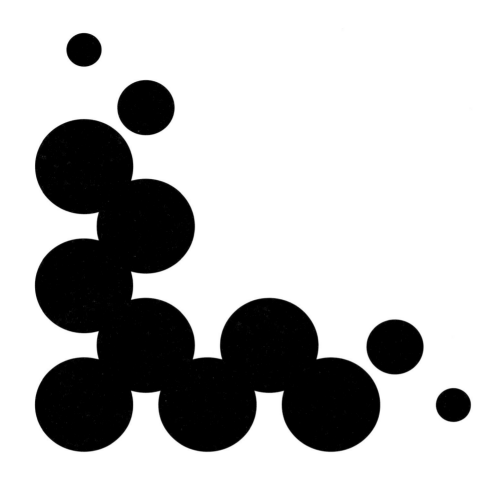

LUCENTUM
1979 · Fernando Medina · Canada

LALEMENT · TRANSPORT
1979 · Wilfried Haest · Belgium

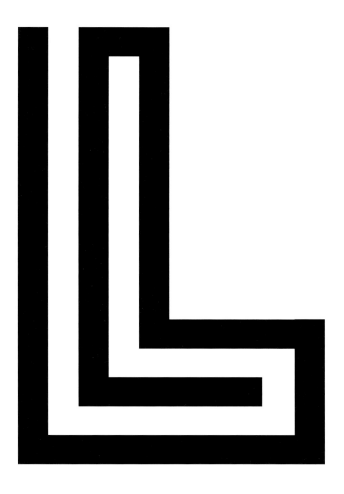

LUHRMANN ARCHITEKTEN · ARCHITECTURE
1958 · Anton Stankowski · Germany

LIBEST · REAL ESTATE
1988 · Katsuichi Ito · Japan

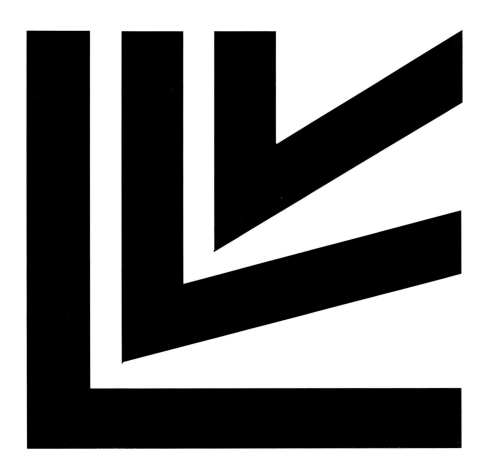

LINEA · ART & DESIGN FAIR
1983 · Paul Ibou · Belgium

MUSEO NACIONAL · MUSEUM
1970 · Félix Beltrán · Cuba

MUSÉES NATIONAUX DE FRANCE · MUSEUMS ORGANISATION
1974 · Adrian Frutiger · Switzerland

MERCATOR PRESS · PUBLISHING
1985 · Paul Ibou · Belgium

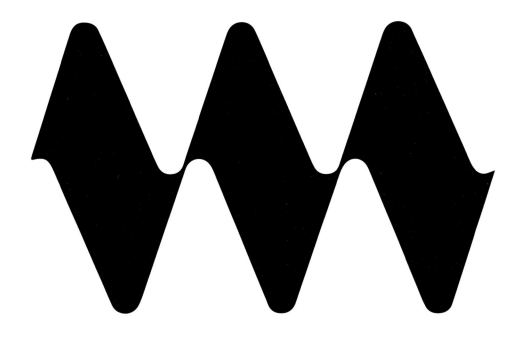

MATCH BOX · DESIGN AGENCY
1983 · Naoki Hiraoka · Japan

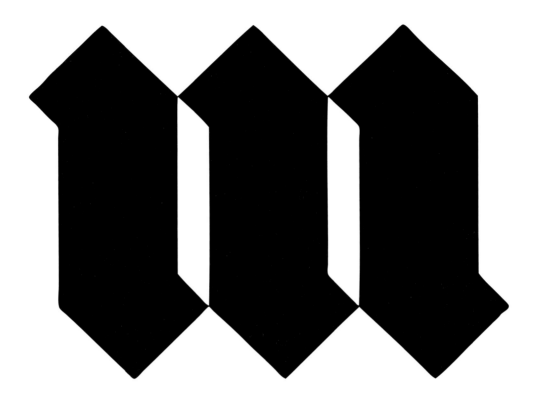

DROGERIE MUFF · PHARMACY
1966 · Atelier Stadelmann Bisig · Switzerland

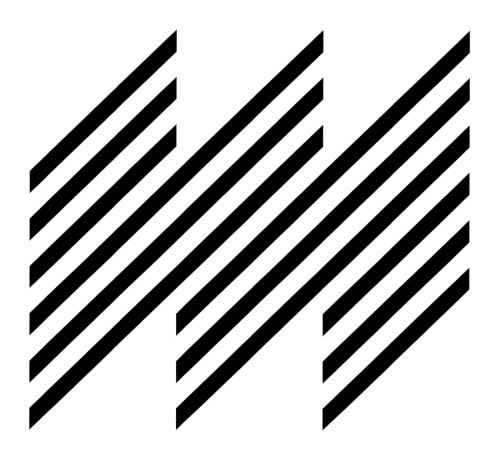

MÉTRO MAGAZINE INC · NEWSSTANDS
1980 · Jacques Roy · Canada

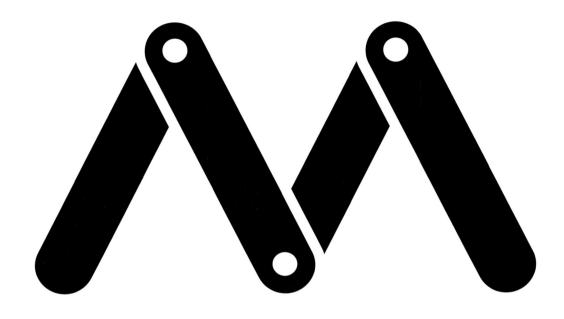

MECADEMIC · ROBOT ARMS
2013 · Ivan Filipov · Bulgaria

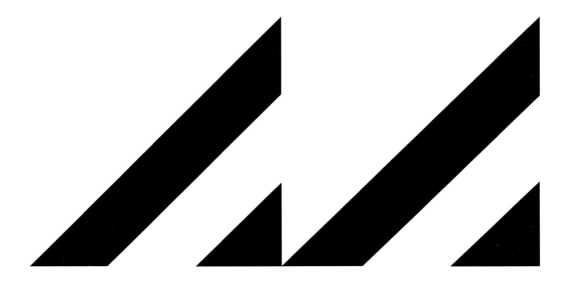

DRUKKERIJ MICHIELS · PRINTING
1975 · Jozef Sprengers · Belgium

MESY SHIRTS · CLOTHING
1974 · Paul Ibou · Belgium

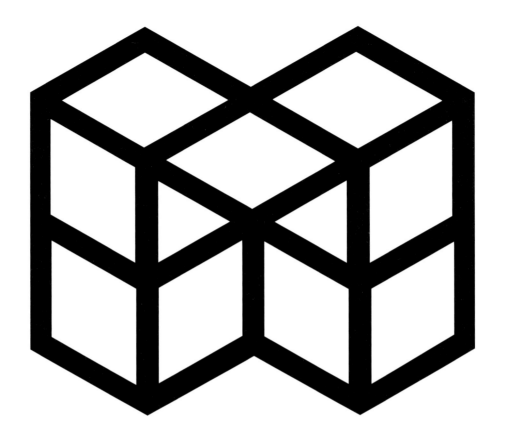

MARUKO BIRUMEN · PROPERTY MANAGEMENT
1977 · Yasaburo Kuwayama · Japan

MIYATA · BEAUTY SALON
1978 · Toshinori Nozaki · Japan

MULTIBANCO MERCANTIL DE MEXICO · BANK
1985 · Jorge Fernandez de la Reguera · Mexico

MAINICHI FUJIN · PUBLISHING
1986 · Yasaburo Kuwayama · Japan

MÄRSTA TRYCK AB · PRINTING
1985 · Hans Kündig · Sweden

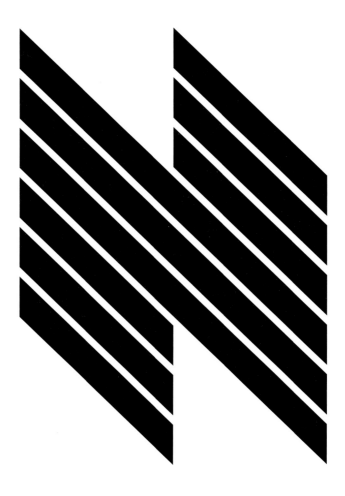

NORTON TRANSPORTACIONES · TRANSPORTATION
1982 · Félix Beltrán · Cuba

NATIONAL BANK OF CANADA · BANK
1979 · Vasco Design · Canada

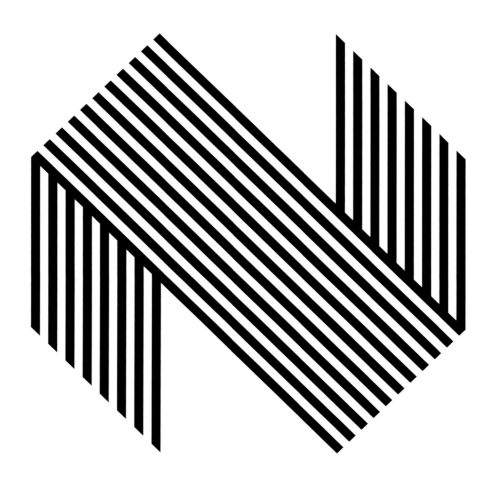

BANCO NOROESTE · BANK
1973 · João Carlos Cauduro, Ludovico Antonio Martino · Brazil

TRANSNITRO · TRANSPORTATION
1972 · Arnold Saks, Karl Hartig · United States of America

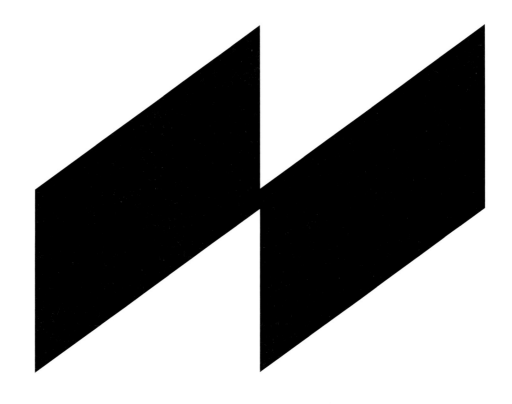

NAGASE RUBBER · SPORTING GOODS
1979 · Kazuo Tajima · Japan

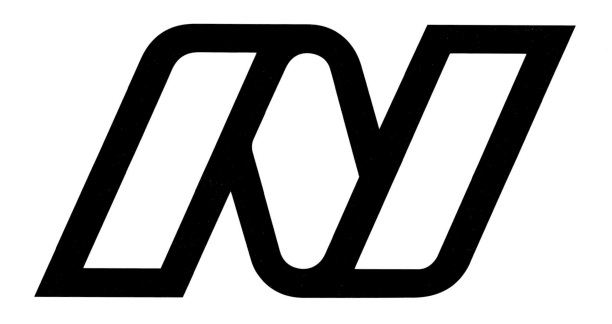

NACIONAL DE RESINAS · PLASTICS
1978 · Jorge Carral, Fernando Rión · Mexico

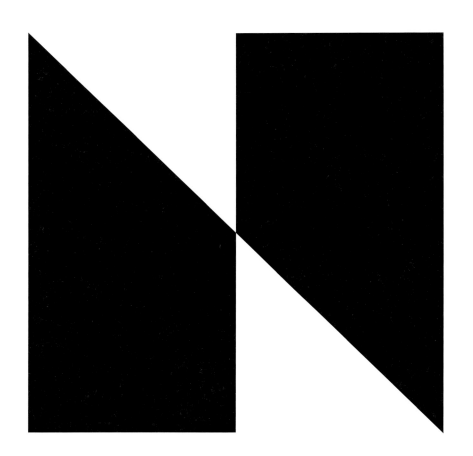

DECIEP
1972 · Félix Beltrán · Cuba

NISHIDA SEISAKUSHO · CERAMICS
1983 · Kazuharu Fujii · Japan

NOTO KANKŌ KAIHATSU
1987 · Kazuhiro Murata · Japan

NORCOUNT PROPERTY DEVELOPMENT · RESIDENTIAL PROPERTY DEVELOPMENT
1975 · Stuart Ash · Canada

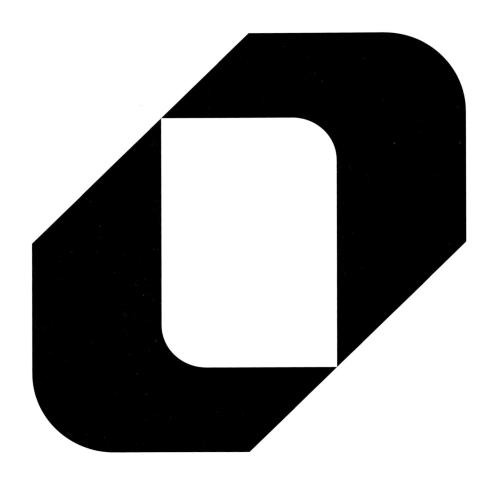

NIHON SHURUI HANBAI · FOODS AND BEVERAGES
1979 · Shigeo Katsuoka · Japan

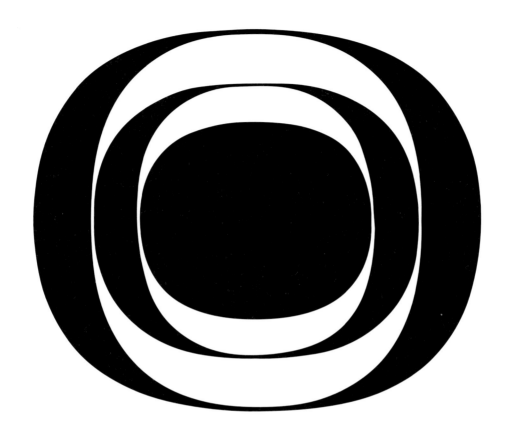

GENESEE HEALTH SYSTEMS · HEALTHCARE
1969 · R. Roger Remington · United States of America

ONTARIO EDUCATIONAL COMMUNICATIONS AUTHORITY
1971 · Burton Kramer · Canada

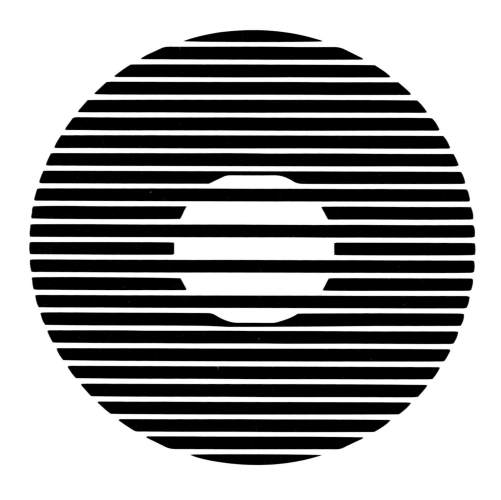

OPTICAL PERIPHERALS LABORATORY · LABORATORY
1982 · Tim Larsen · United States of America

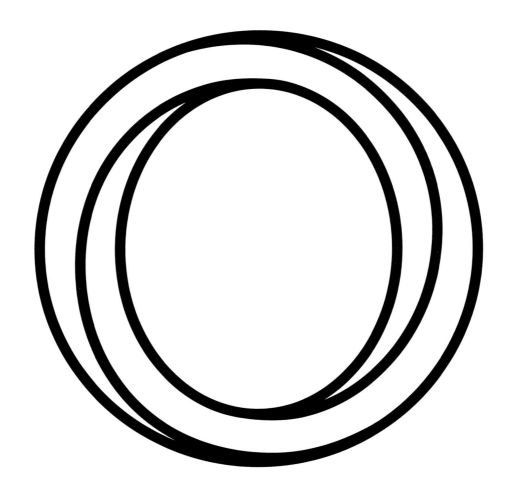

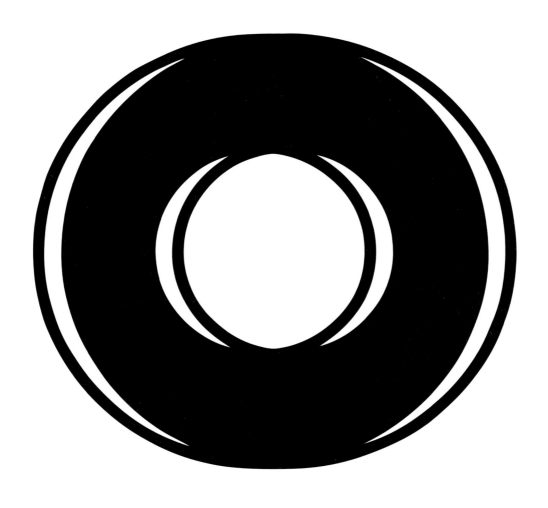

MACQUARIE BANK · BANK
1984 · Cato Partners · Australia

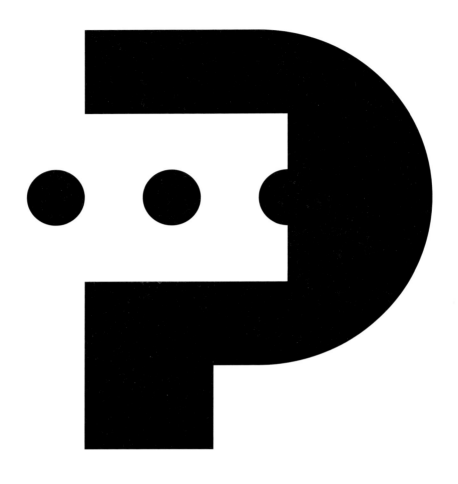

PAYDRO · TICKETING
2016 · Jeroen van Eerden · The Netherlands

PERCEPTIVE PRESS · BOOK PUBLISHING
2015 · MashCreative · United Kingdom

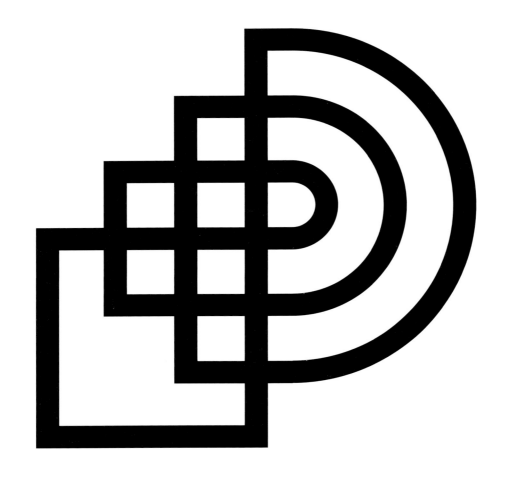

PETERSON PROPERTIES · REAL ESTATE
1985 · Steven Rousso · United States of America

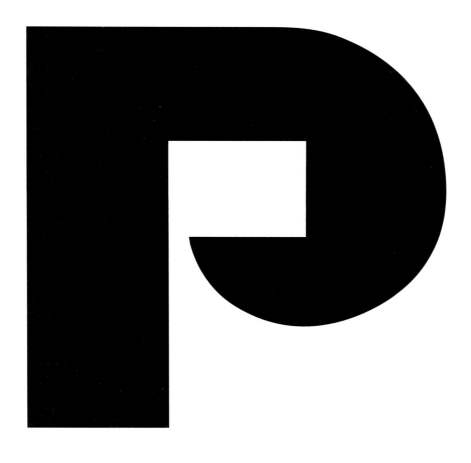

PALACE SHIPPING · SHIPPING
1973 · Katsumi Nagata, Yasaburo Kuwayama · Japan

PHOTOCOMPO CENTER · TYPESETTING
1970 · Paul Ibou · Belgium

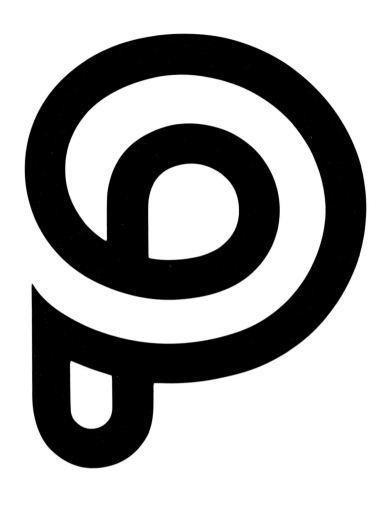

PACIFIC FUEL TRADING · FUEL
1983 · Tatsuhito Yamamoto · Japan

PUOLIMATKA CORPORATION · CONSTRUCTION
1981 · Esko Miettinen · Finland

PRANTL & SÖHNE · FORWARDING AGENCY
1985 · Othmar Motter · Austria

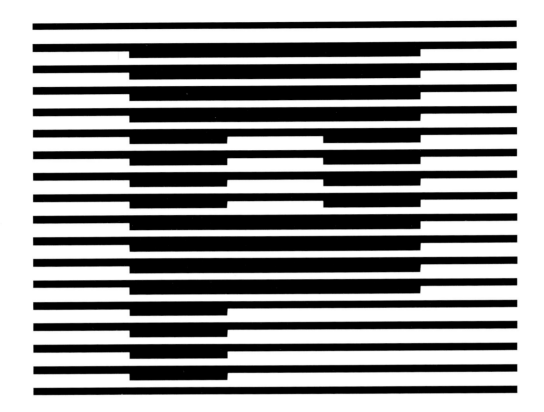

PITTOORS · VIDEO CENTER
1984 · Paul Ibou · Belgium

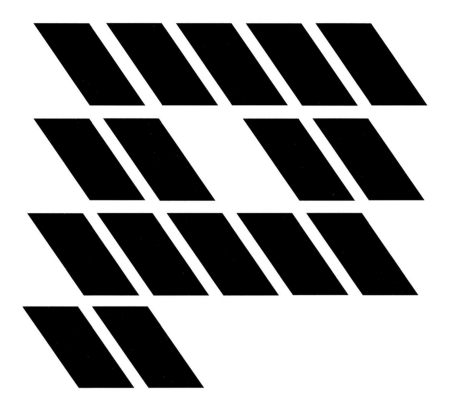

PEETERS · ROOFING
1989 · Paul Ibou · Belgium

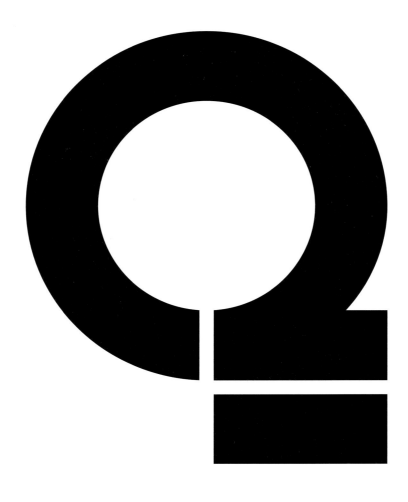

COMMISSION DES DROITS DE LA PERSONNE DU QUÉBEC
1984 · Raymond Bellemare · Canada

GRUPO RENOVACION · INSTITUTE OF SOCIOLOGY
1970 · Álvaro Sotillo · Venezuela

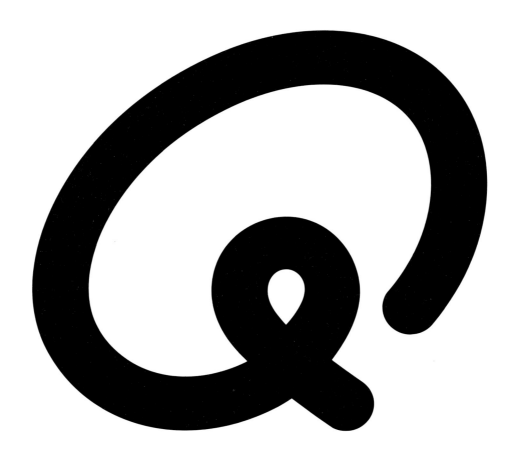

Q MUSIC · RADIO & TELEVISION STATION
2015 · DixonBaxi · United Kingdom

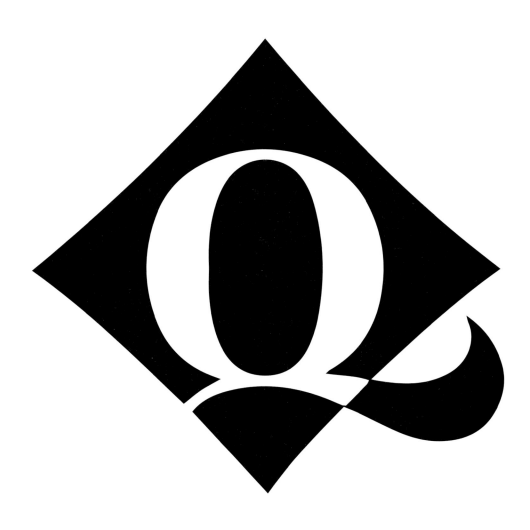

TYPOGRAPHERS INTERNATIONAL ASSOCIATION
1987 · Hermann Zapf · Germany

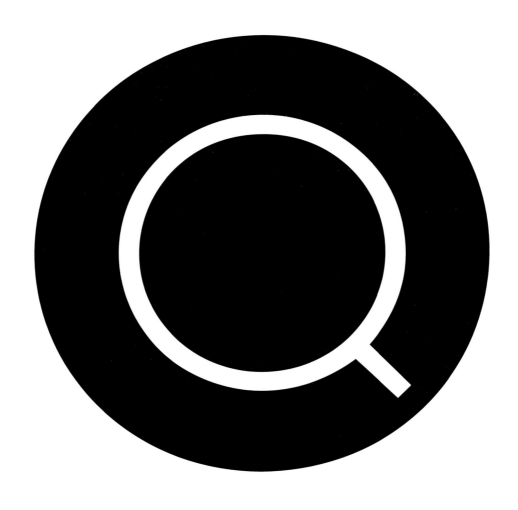

QUICK MAID · COFFEE VENDING MACHINERY
1980 · Norman Moore · United Kingdom

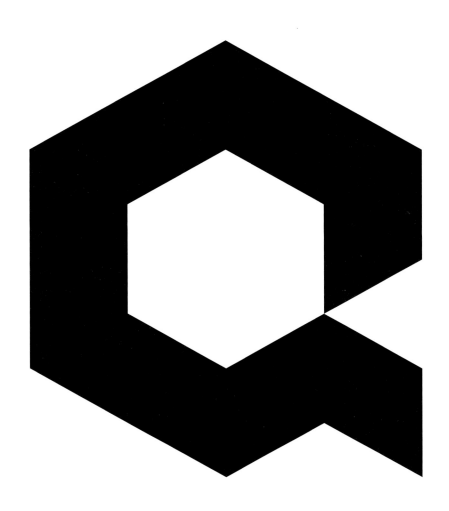

QUIXEL · SOFTWARE & TECHNOLOGY
2013 · 1910 Design & Communication · Sweden

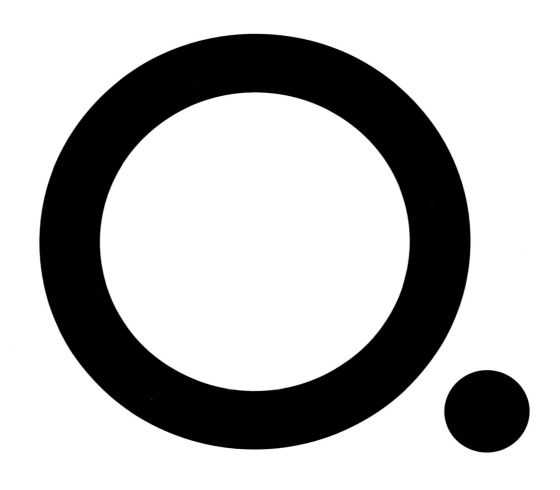

QUANTUMIZE · COACHING & CONSULTING
2010 · Today · Belgium

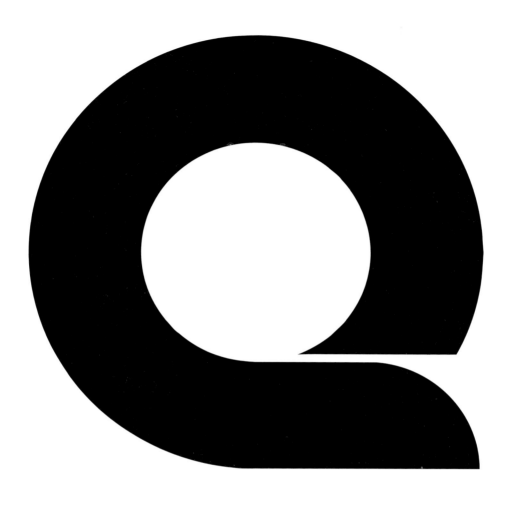

QUEBEC DIESEL · CASTING REPAIRS
1969 · Pierre Pelletier · Canada

ROPAN FILMS · FILM PRODUCTION
1976 · Sudarshan Dheer · India

RANSON · PROPERTY
2014 · SocioDesign · United Kingdom

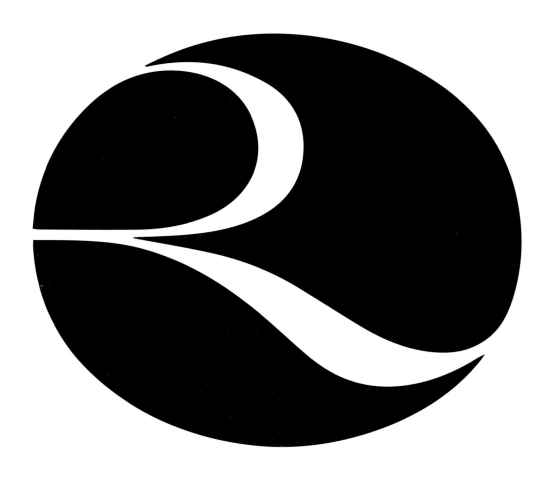

RYUKYUS · BANK
1979 · Yasaburo Kuwayama · Japan

REGENT INTERNATIONAL · HOTEL CHAIN
1979 · Armando Milani · Italy

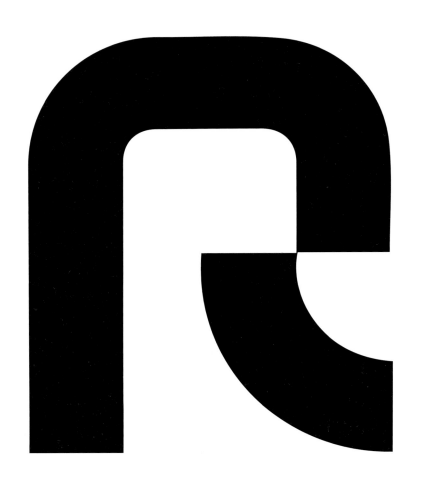

REVI
Frank Maes · Belgium

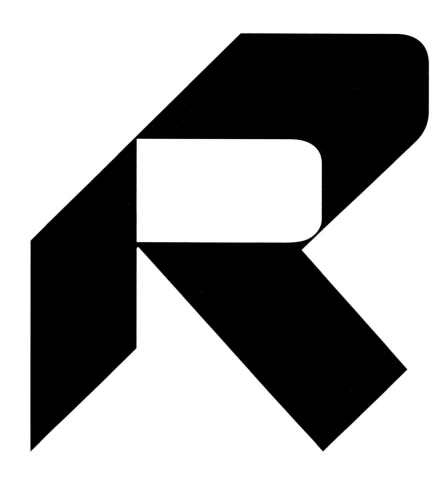

REFLEX DESIGN · DESIGN STUDIO
1981 · Armando Milani · Italy

RELIANCE STEEL · METAL PROCESSING
1971 · Jerome Jensik · United States of America

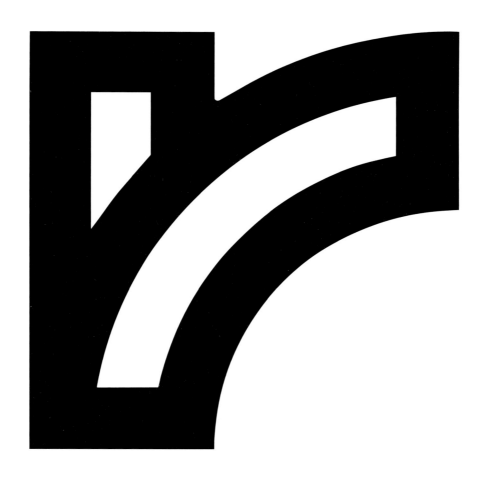

REINE CLAUDE · LADIES APPAREL
1985 · Fumio Imura · Japan

MUSÉE RODIN PARIS · ART MUSEUM
1980 · Adrian Frutiger · Switzerland

R STAR
2012 · Bohdan Harbaruk · Ukraine

RIBBON · PHARMACY
1979 · Giancarlo Iliprandi · Italy

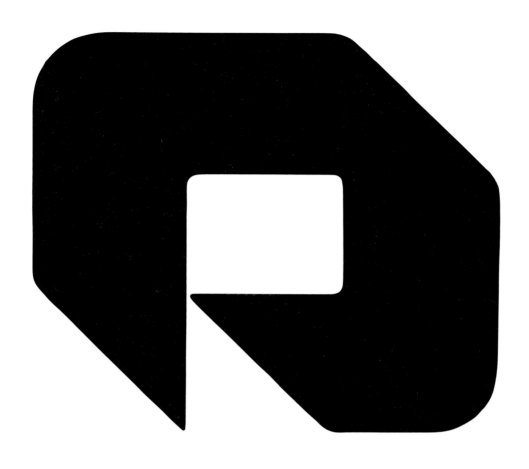

REED PAPER CORPORATION
1975 · Burton Kramer · Canada

SELLTRON SOLAR ILLUMINATION · MANUFACTURER
2017 · Shreyas Ashok Bendre · India

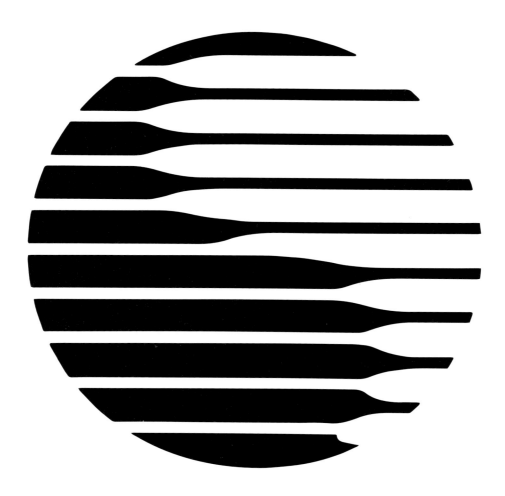

SCITECH CENTRE · PHARMACEUTICAL MANUFACTURER
1988 · Sudarshan Dheer · India

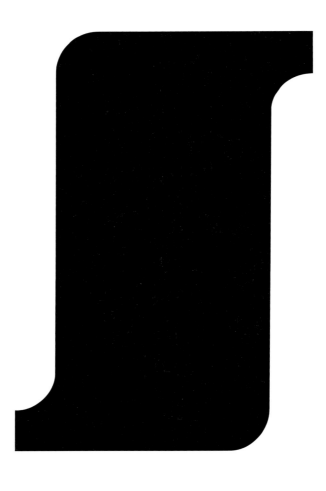

SLEURS · IMPORT & EXPORT
1967 · Ravan · Belgium

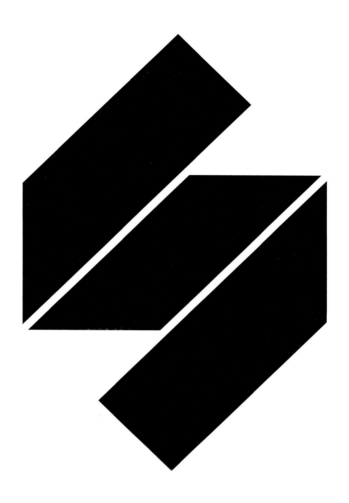

SMET · DRILLING
Ludo Feyen · Belgium

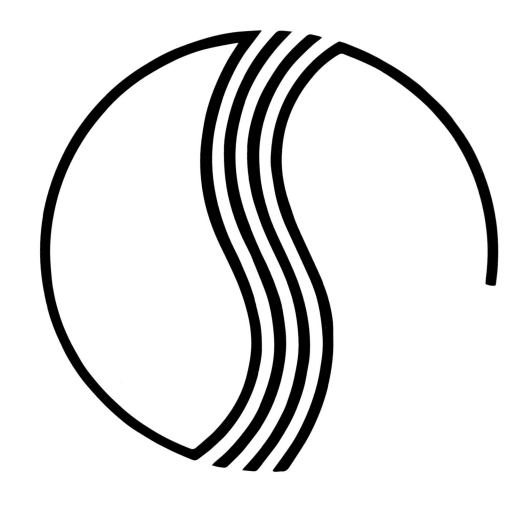

STYLE ASIA LIMITED · MANUFACTURER
1978 · Sudarshan Dheer · India

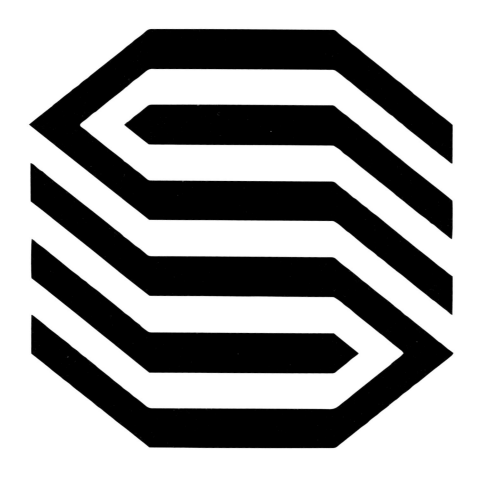

STORWAL · OFFICE STORAGE UNITS
1982 · Burton Kramer · Canada

SPAARKREDIET · SAVINGS BANK
1982 · Paul Ibou · Belgium

BOENEN · INVESTING
1988 · Roger Vansevenant · Belgium

SEDGEFORD SOUNDS · MUSIC INDUSTRY
2013 · MashCreative · United Kingdom

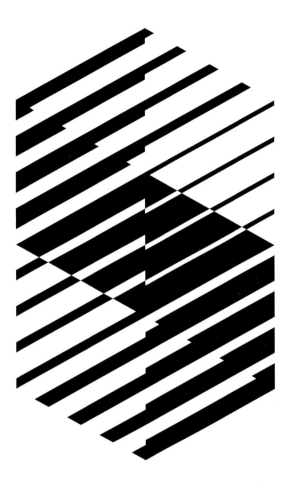

GROUPE SÉGUIN INGÉNÉRIE
1984 · Raymond Bellemare · Canada

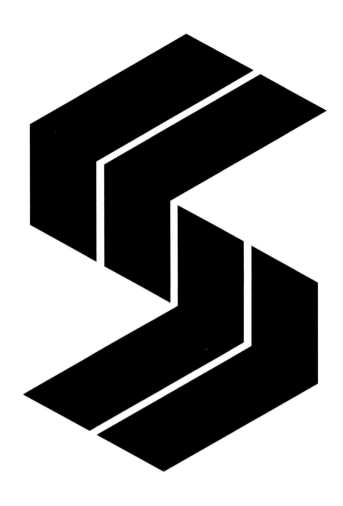

STATE FEDERAL SAVINGS & LOAN · BANK
Davies Kaufmann Inc · United States of America

STOMA-CLUB
Fernand Bernaerts · Belgium

SWISS CREDIT BANK · BANK
Adolf Flückiger, B.E. Rosshäusem · Switzerland

SEXTRA · FILM EDITING
1968 · Paul Ibou · Belgium

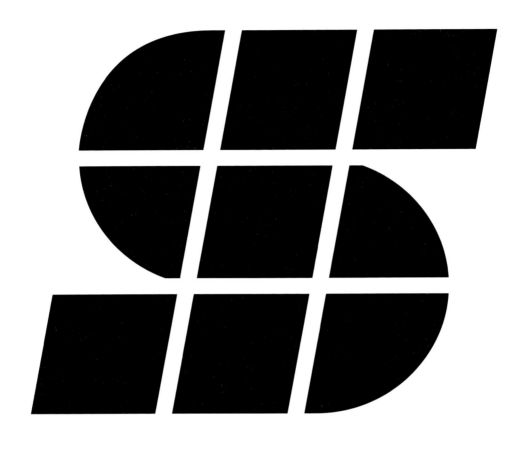

SOLEIN · SOLAR ENERGY
2017 · Risto Pärtin (Friik) · Estonia

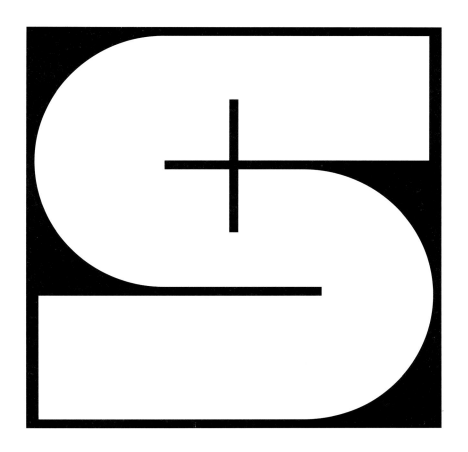

SERVIPLUS
1970 · Pierre Fluery · Canada

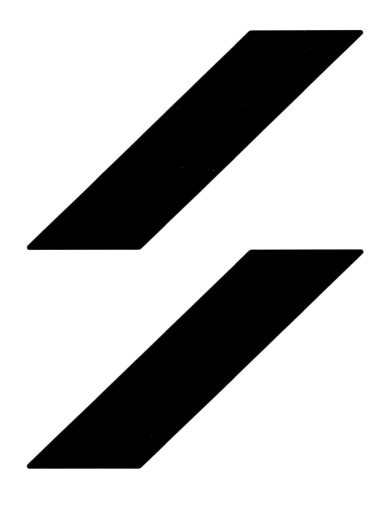

SOGIPLAST · PLASTICS
1982 · A. Ubertazzi, D. Soffientini, R. Nava · Italy

SECURITY FIRST NATIONAL BANK · BANK
1966 · Saul Bass · United States of America

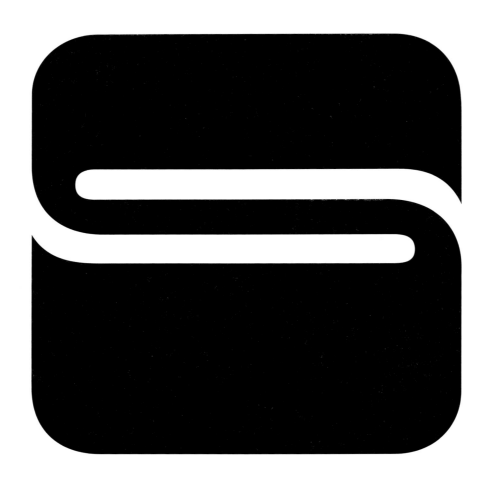

SCHWARZ
1970 · Angelo Sganzerla · Italy

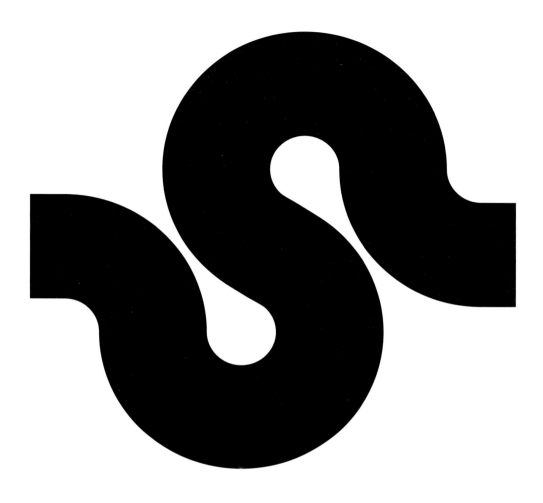

TRANSPORT SUDBURY · PUBLIC TRANSPORT
1972 · Stuart Ash · Canada

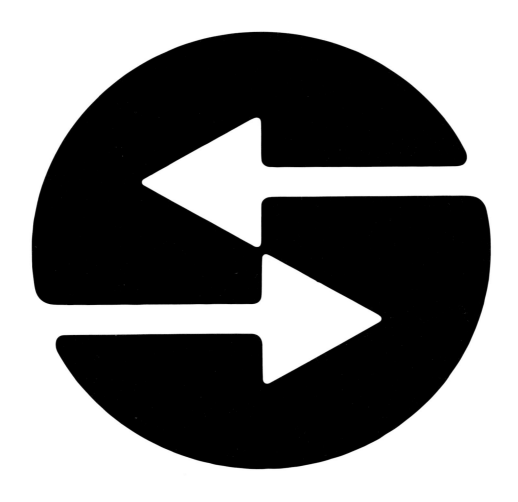

PROJECT SCHOOL TO SCHOOL
1969 · Burton Kramer · Canada

SURFACING · TEXTILE DESIGN & EXHIBITION
1972 · Burton Kramer · Canada

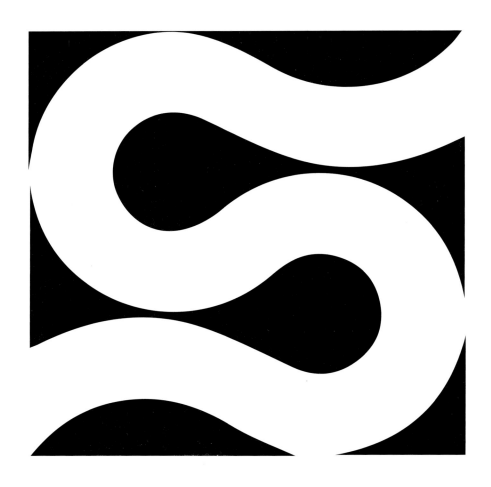

SAKAMOTO PRINTING · PRINTING
1977 · Kazuharu Fujii · Japan

SOFTWARE INTERNATIONAL · COMPUTER SOFTWARE
1978 · Morfos Diseño · Mexico

TOKYO CENTRAL MUSEUM · MUSEUM
1971 · Kazumasa Nagai · Japan

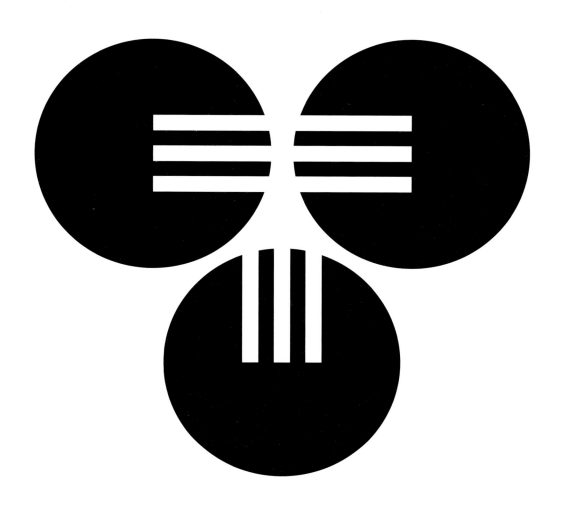

TRENDGROWTH TRANS · TRADING
Eduardo Andrés Cánovas · Argentina

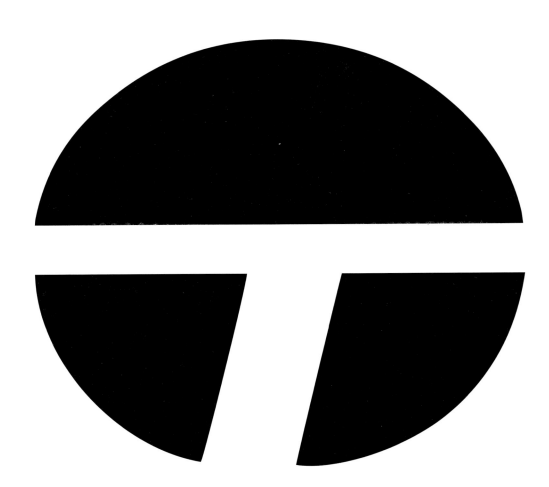

THE TRAVEL SHOKAI · TRAVEL COUNSELOR
1986 · Yūji Nagai, Keizō Murotani · Japan

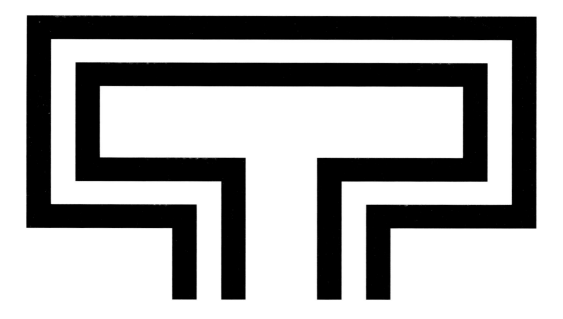

GALLERY TRAZO · ART GALLERY
Félix Beltrán · Cuba

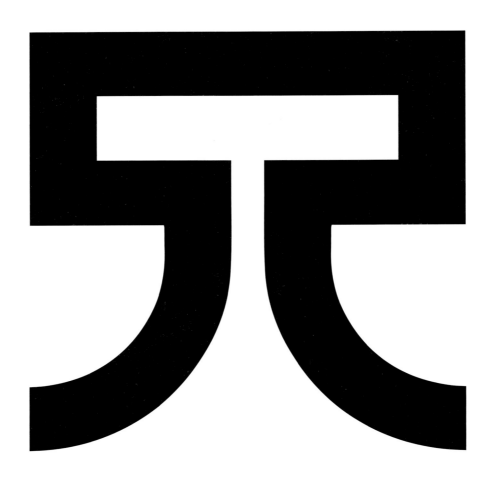

TALENT · MUSIC ASSOCIATION
1981 · Paul Ibou · Belgium

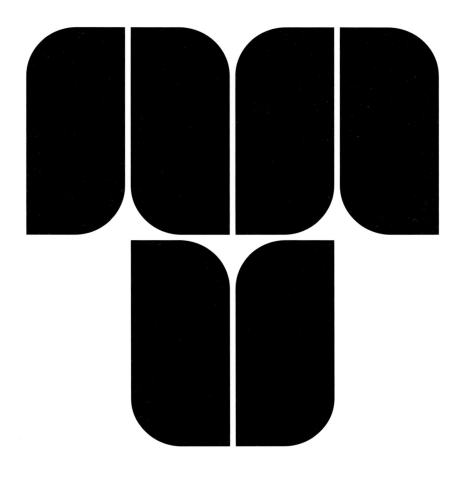

TRICOTEUSE
1968 · Roger Baert · Belgium

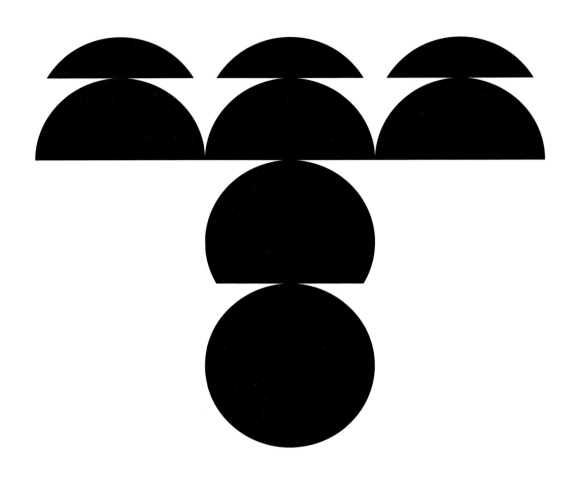

TACHÉ · JEWELRY
1973 · Paul Ibou · Belgium

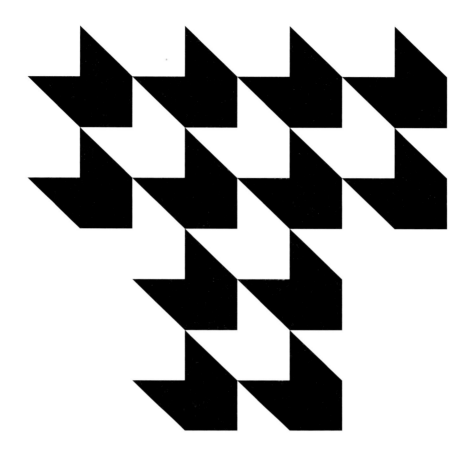

THE TREE HOUSE · PROPERTY
2014 · MashCreative · United Kingdom

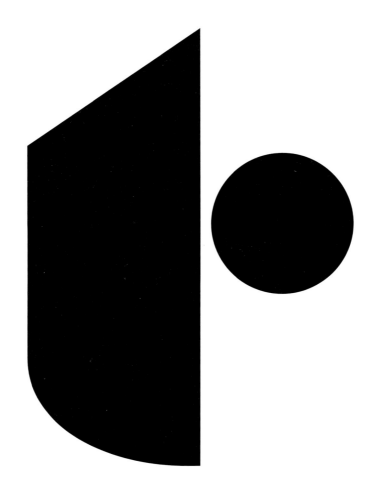

TASKERS · WORKFORCE SOLUTIONS & RECRUITMENT
2011 · Boy Bastiaens · The Netherlands

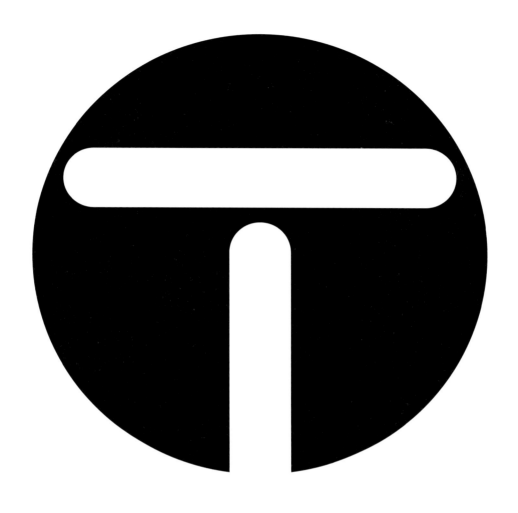

HONG KONG TELEPHONE COMPANY · TELECOMMUNICATIONS
1978 · Henry Steiner · Austria

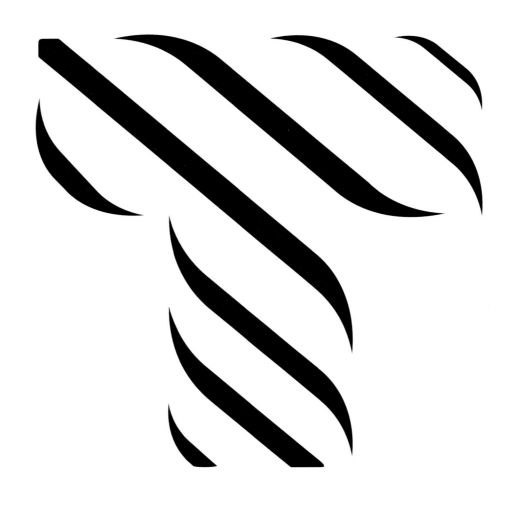

TURN · MARKETING AGENCY
2012 · MashCreative · United Kingdom

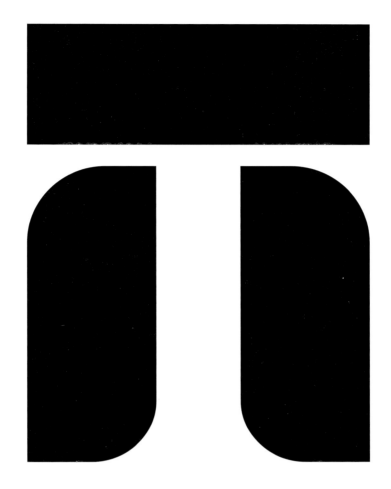

TOM TRAMEL
1977 · Jean-Claude Müller · United States of America

TORONTO OLYMPIC BID · OLYMPICS
1996 · Stuart Ash · Canada

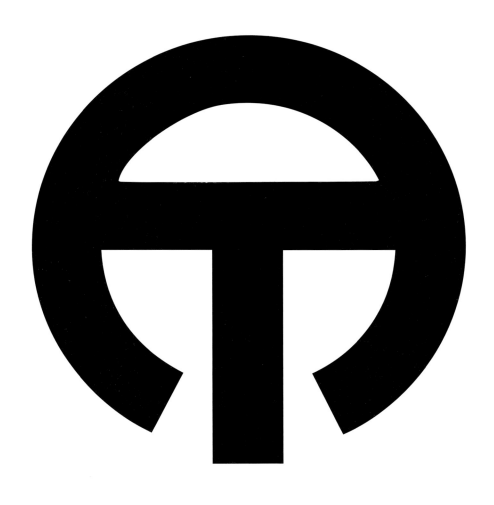

ANTWERP TAX · TAXI COMPANY
1967 · Paul Ibou · Belgium

TRADE UNION SPORTS ORGANISATIONS
1986 · Ramis Guseinov · USSR (Russia)

URBANET CORPORATION · REAL ESTATE
1987 · Shigeo Katsuoka · Japan

UNIREP · GRAPHIC PRODUCTION CENTER
1970 · Paul Ibou · Belgium

UNIVERSITY OF ANTWERP · EDUCATION
2005 · KAN · Belgium

UNITEX · IMPORT & EXPORT
1982 · Edi Berk · Slovenia

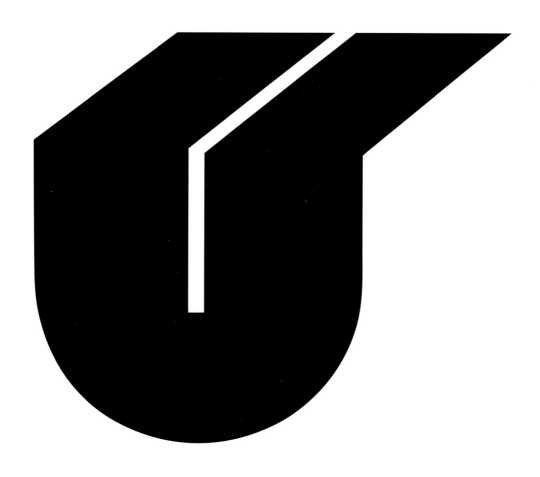

ULSHORE · PHARMACEUTICALS
1981 · Maurizio Milani · Italy

MODE U · APPAREL
1986 · Takeshi Otaka · Japan

UNIPROD · COMMUNITY SUPPORT
1983 · Karol Śliwka · Poland

UNITED AIRLINES · AIRLINE
1974 · Saul Bass & Associates · United States of America

UNITY BANK · BANK
1974 · Gregory Fossella Associates · United States of America

UNIVERSAL · TRAVEL AGENCY
1971 · Jean Delaunay · France

UPPSTART CONFERENCE · CONFERENCE
2016 · 1910 Design & Communication · Sweden

URBATIQUE QUEBEC · URBAN ENGINEERING
1969 · Yvon Laroche · Canada

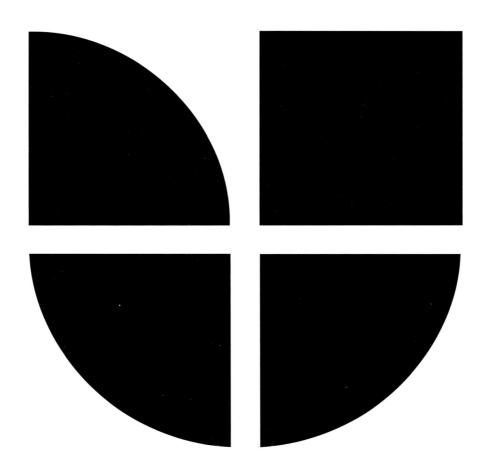

UNIVISION · TELEVISION NETWORK
1989 · Ivan Chermayeff, Tom Geismar · United States of America

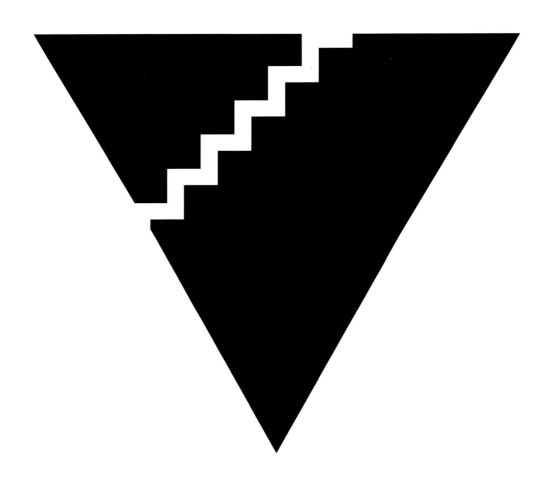

KONSTRUKCJA W PROCESIE
1990 · Sławomir Iwański · Poland

VOICECON · CONFERENCE
2018 · Chris Logsdon · United States of America

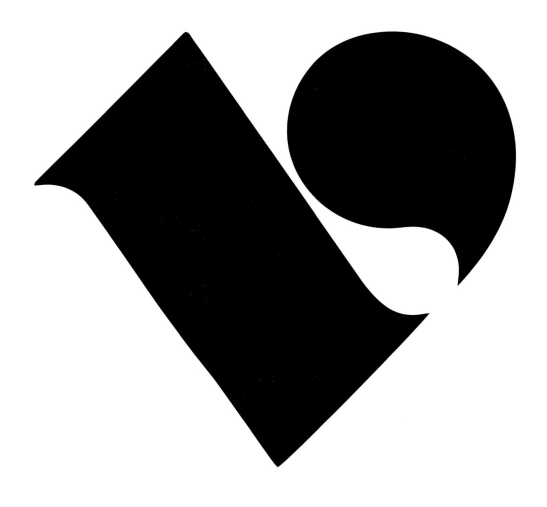

VANESSA LADIES' CLOTHING · CLOTHING
1979 · Othmar Motter · Austria

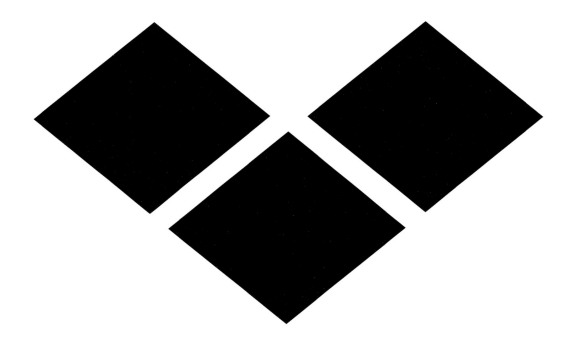

LOGO CENTER INTERECHO
1986 · Paul Ibou · Belgium

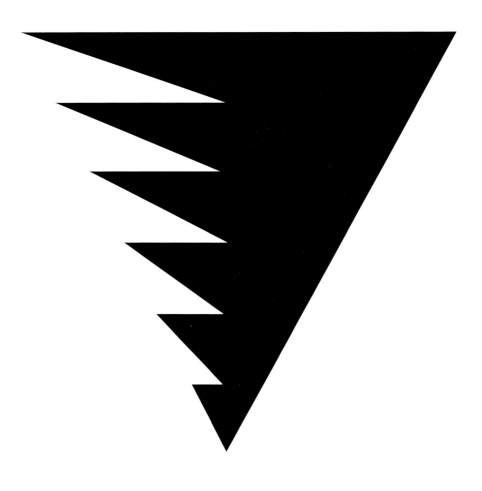

VDK SPAARBANK · BANK
Paul Ibou · Belgium

VOZILA GORICA · AUTOMOBILES
1963 · Oskar Kogoj · Yugoslavia (Slovenia)

BOUTIQUE VERONIKA · BOUTIQUE
1980 · Othmar Motter · Austria

SWISS VOLKSBANK · BANK
Jäggi Dieter AG · Switzerland

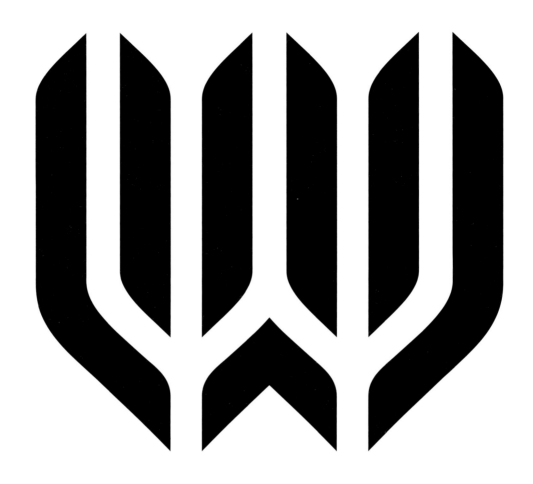

WASHINGTON MUTUAL SAVINGS · BANK
1968 · Ken Parkhurst · United States of America

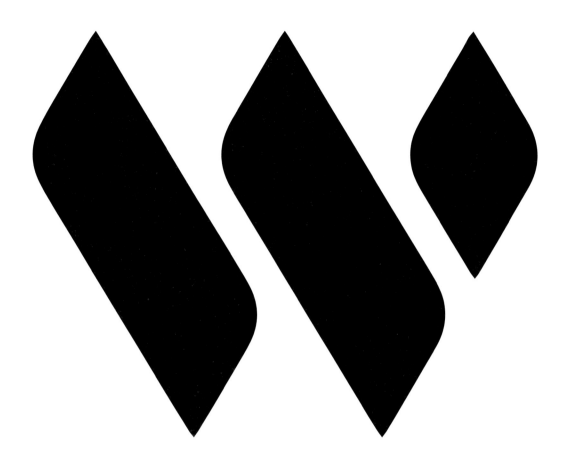

WELLMART · GROCERY CHAIN
1982 · Akira Hirata, Koji Mori · Japan

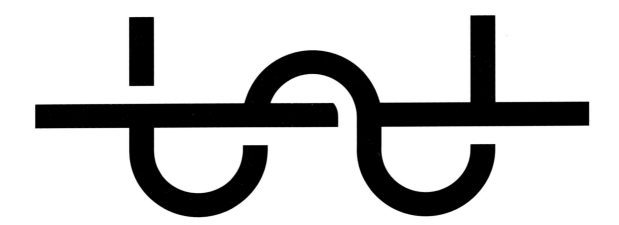

WILFRIDS · BARBER
2016 · Jared Granger · United States of America

WESTMARK HOTELS · HOTEL
1984 · Steve Rousso · United States of America

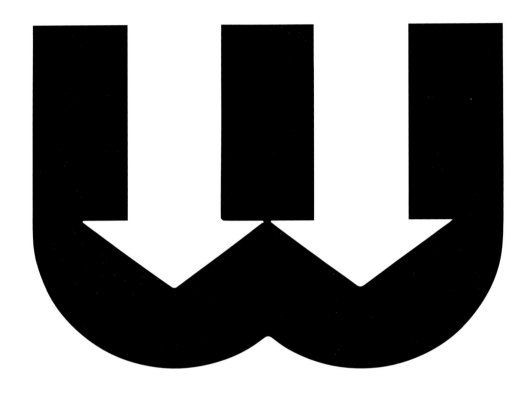

YOUR WAY · BOOKSHOP
1974 · Erik De Meyer · Belgium

WARNER COMMUNICATIONS · ENTERTAINMENT GROUP
1974 · Saul Bass & Associates · United States of America

WATERMAN · FOUNTAIN PENS
1983 · Rudi Meyer · Switzerland

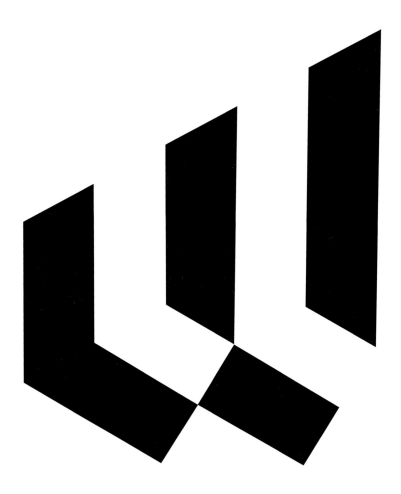

WITHERSPOON DESIGN · DESIGN CONSULTANT
1982 · Randy Lynn Witherspoon · United States of America

FIRST WISCONSIN · BANK
Landor Associates · United States of America

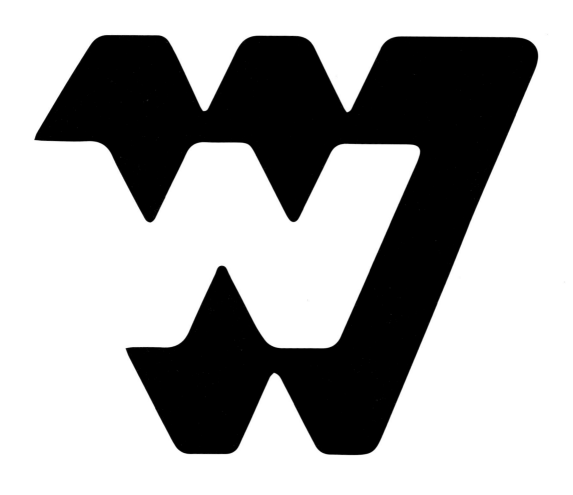

WANNER · EXCAVATORS
1981 · Peter G. Ulmer · Switzerland

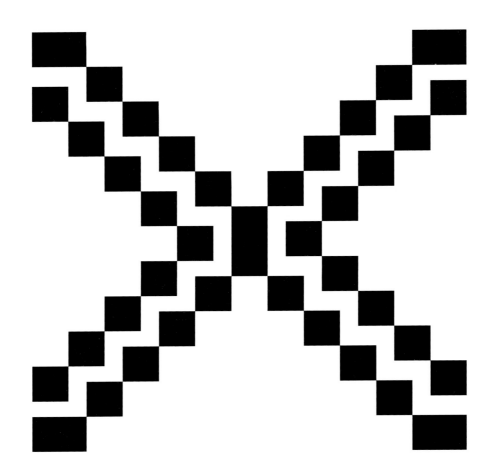

WORKGROUP TEXT INTERECHO
1984 · Paul Ibou · Belgium

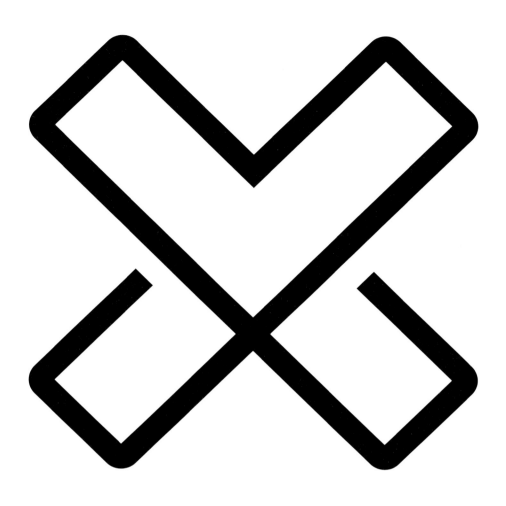

VAYNERX · COMMUNICATIONS
2017 · Chris Logsdon · United States of America

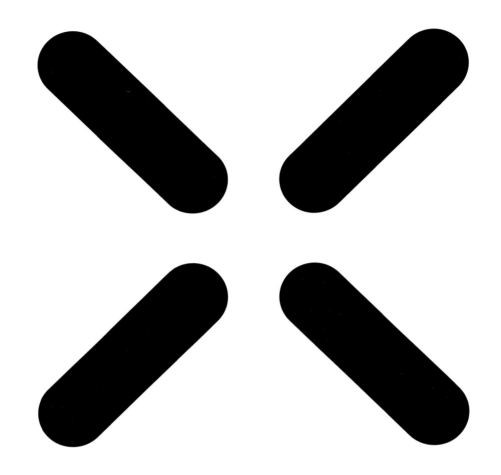

XENEX · HEALTHCARE
2014 · Jonathan Lawrence (Matchstic) · United States of America

EDITORIAL TIEMPO NUEVO · PUBLISHING
1970 · John Lange · Venezuela

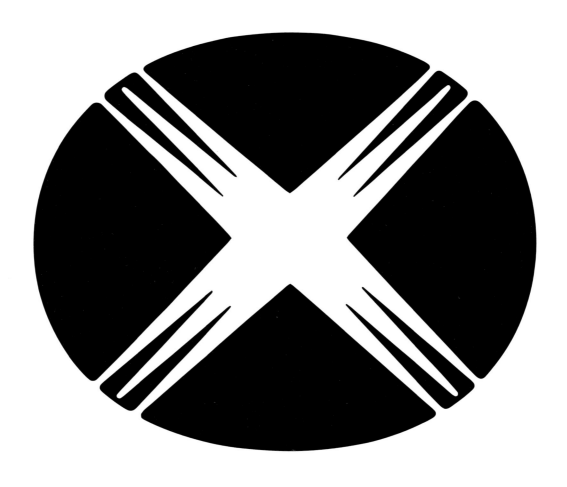

FUJI XEROX RYUTSU INC · BUSINESS SERVICES & DIGITAL PRINTING SOLUTIONS
1985 · Katsuichi Ito · Japan

INTERNOST RX SYSTEMS
Frank Maes · Belgium

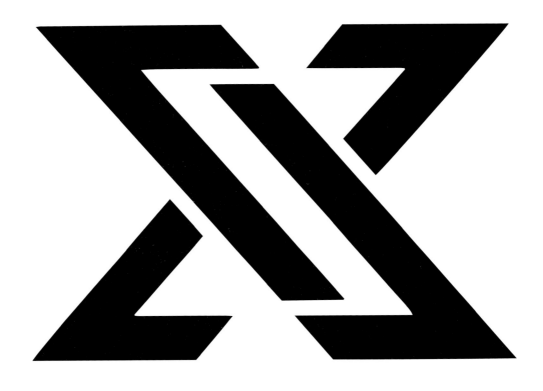

X RENT-A-CAR · CAR RENTAL
1986 · Hiroko Horimoto · Japan

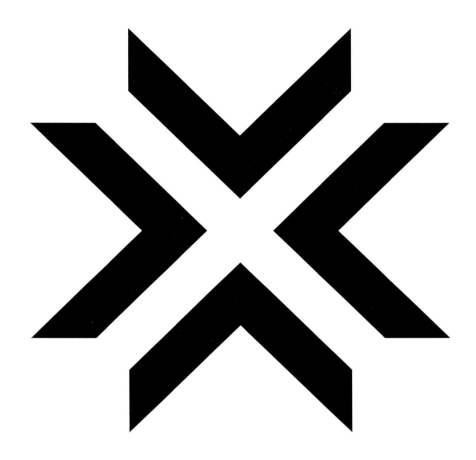

BLACK WATCH GLOBAL · INTELLIGENCE AND RISK MANAGEMENT CONSULTANCY
2009 · MashCreative · United Kingdom

YASUDA TRUST BANK · BANK
1974 · Kazumasa Nagai · Japan

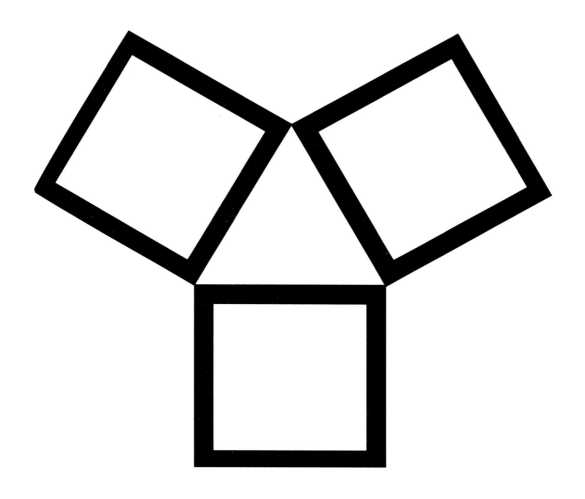

MUSEUM OF ART YOKOHAMA · MUSEUM
Masaharu Takata · Japan

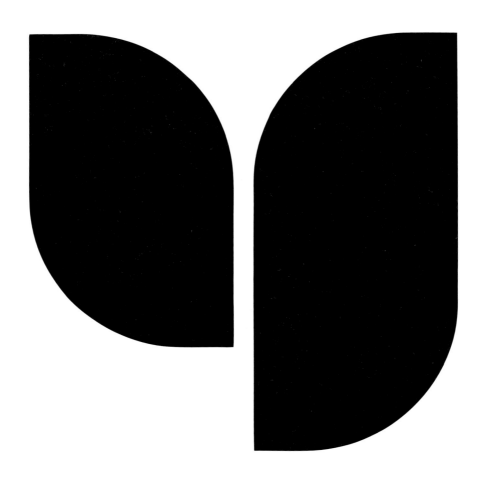

YUASA BEAUTY PARLOR · COSMETICS
1977 · Masaaki Ishii · Japan

USPEC · CERAMICS
1972 · Stefan Kanchev · Bulgaria

YTONG STEEL
1966 · Burton Kramer · Canada

YUYO KŌGYŌ · REAL ESTATE
1986 · Takashi Adachi · Japan

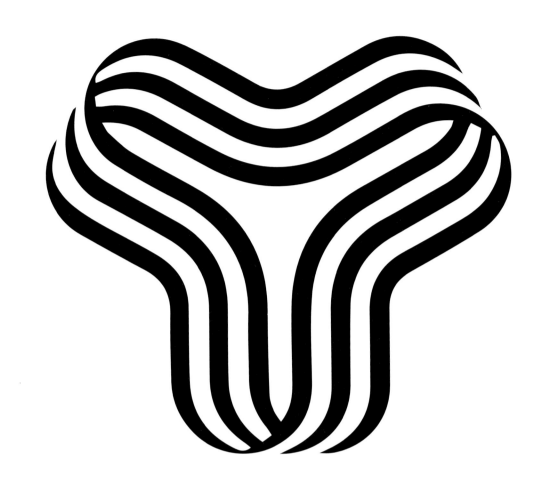

YAMADA CO. · TEXTILES
1974 · Akisato Ueda · Japan

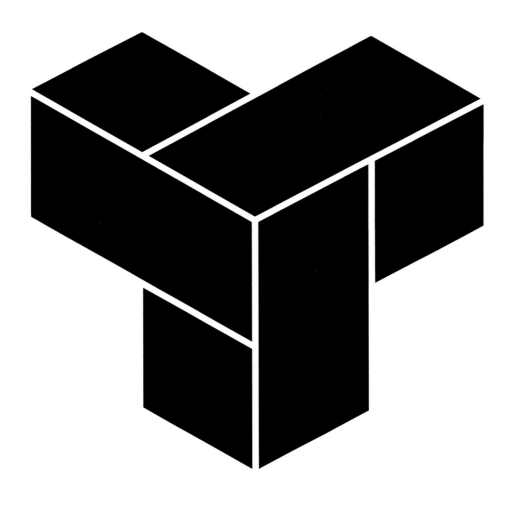

YORK CENTRE · SHOPPING CENTER
1967 · Stuart Ash · Canada

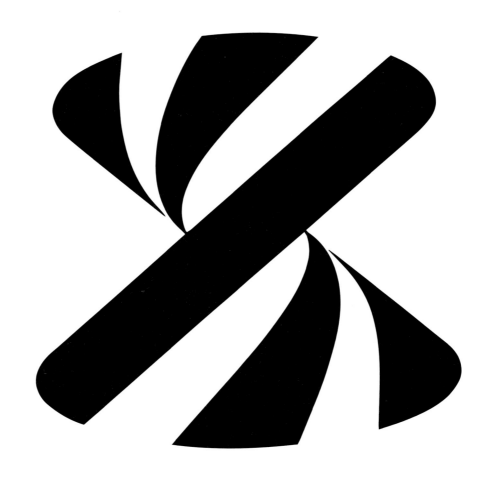

ZENSHINREN · BANK
Katsuichi Ito · Japan

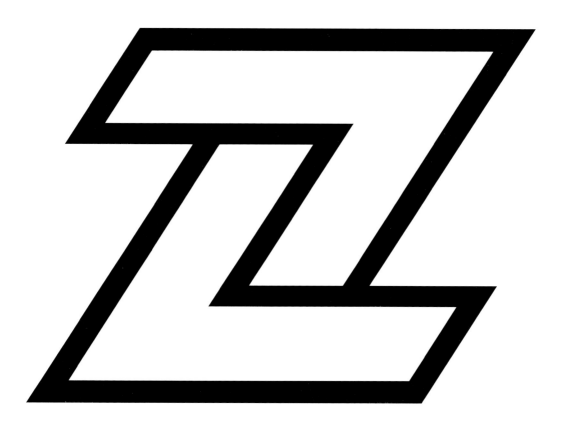

ZEROWATT · ELECTRONICS
1978 · Armando Milani, Maurizio Milani · Italy

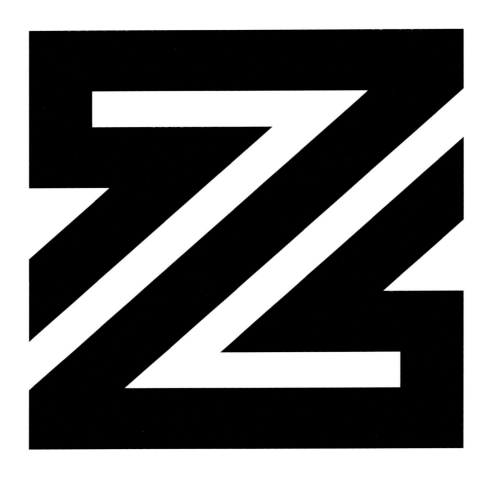

THEREALIST SHOP
2017 · Kakha Kakhadze · Georgia

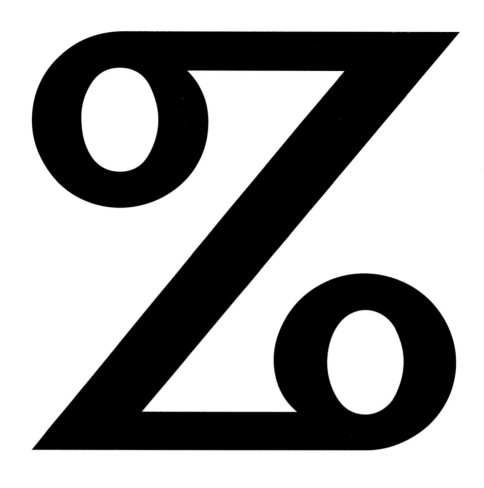

ZUGER KANTONALBANK · BANK
Hans Hartmann · Switzerland

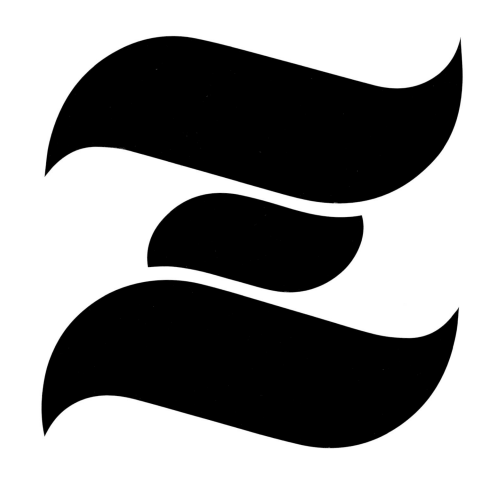

ZEEMAR
1982 · Studio Meersman · Belgium

ZINDER · JEWELRY
1982 · Jorge Reyes · Mexico

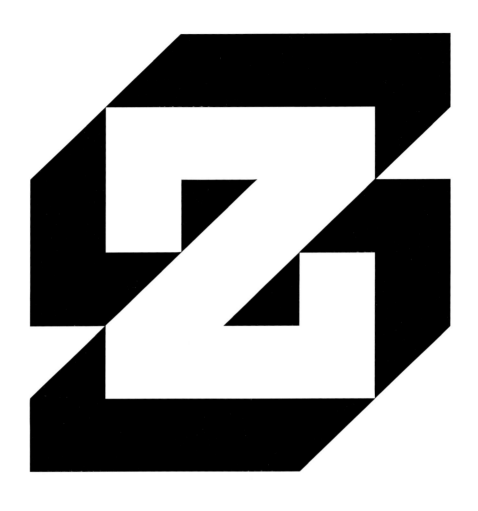

BANCO ZARAGOZANO · BANK
1999 · Cruz Novillo · Spain

VOLKER ZAHM WERBEAGENTUR · ADVERTISING
1960 · Volker Zahm · Germany

ZAMORANO PELUQUERO
1970 · Cruz Novillo · Spain

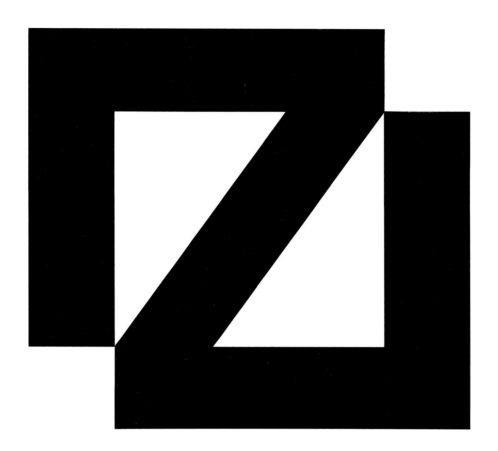

ZINGG
1962 · Werner Mühlemann · Germany

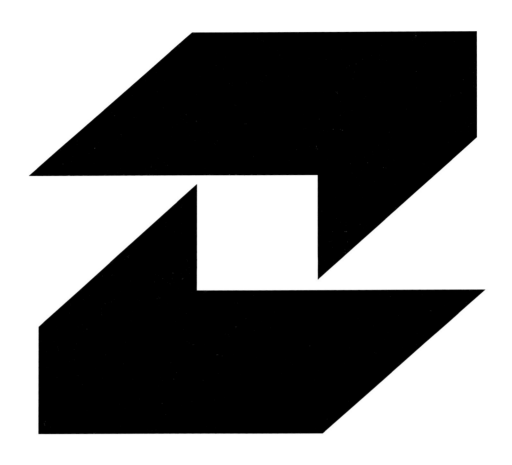

ZÜRCHER ZIEGELEIEN · BRICKS
1963 · Jörg Hamburger · Switzerland

ZÜRICH VERSICHERUNGSGESELLSCHAFT · INSURANCE
1971 · Jörg Hamburger · Switzerland

INDEX

1910 Design & Communication 203, 267

A
Adachi, Takashi 301
Andries, Tom 18
Annerel, Rik 110
Ash, Stuart 32, 181, 237, 254, 303
Atelier Stadelmann Bisig 162
Averink, Leen 59

B
Baert, Roger 247
Bass, Saul 235, 264, 283
Bastiaens, Boy 135, 136, 250
Bellemare, Raymond 198, 227
Beltrán, Félix 22, 27, 82, 106, 118, 158, 172, 178, 245
Bendre, Shreyas Ashok 218
Berk, Edi 130, 260
Bernaerts, Fernand 229
Biemann, Emil O. 101
Bind, Raju D. 133
Binneweg, Herbert 126
Brady, W.H. 25
Breker, Walter 142

C
Cánovas, Eduardo Andrés 243
Carral, Jorge 177
Castro, Dicken 48
Cato Partners 72, 187
Cauduro, João Carlos 174
Chavan, Ajit S. 133
Chermayeff, Ivan 107, 141, 269
Crouwel, Wim 83

D
Dalton, Duane 20, 69
Danziger, Louis 84
Davies Kaufmann Inc 228
De Baudringhien, Filip 77
Debrouwer, Guy 56
de la Reguera, Jorge Fernandez 169

Delaunay, Jean 266
De Meyer, Erik 14, 282
De Pauw, Francis 19
De Pelseneer, E. 95
de Santis, Alfredo 71
Dheer, Sudarshan 206, 219, 222
Dieter AG, Jäggi 277
Dirix, Francis 41, 94
DixonBaxi 79, 200
Doolittle, Douglas 52

E
Eisenmenger, Friedrich 150
Engle, Ray 86

F
Ferraro Senior, Armando 112
Feyen, Ludo 221
Filipov, Ivan 164
Fletcher, Alan 75
Flückiger, Adolf 230
Fluery, Pierre 233
Fretz, Glenn 120
Friik 232
Frutiger, Adrian 13, 121, 159, 214
Fujii, Kazuharu 179, 240
Fukano, Toshio 88
Fuller, Scott 80

G
Gallo, Gerald 70
Geismar, Tom 107, 141, 269
Geisser, Robert 100
Goldsmith, William H. 53
Gonzalez Ruiz, Guillermo 123
Granger, Jared 280
Graphic Controls Corporation 96
Gregory Fossella Associates 265
Grözinger, Klaus 99
Guseinov, Ramis 256

H
Hadlač, Jiří 31

Haest, Wilfried 154
Hamburger, Jörg 314, 315
Harbaruk, Bohdan 215
Harder, Rolf 51
Hartig, Karl 175
Hartmann, Hans 307
Hayez Drukkers 78
Hergenröther, Walter 104
Hiraoka, Naoki 161
Hirata, Akira 33, 279
Hirose, Ken'ichi 62
Hollick, Kenneth 146
Horimoto, Hiroko 294
Hosokawa, Mitsuo 140

I
Ibou, Paul 10, 12, 23, 38, 39, 44, 55, 57, 65, 73, 76, 97, 98, 116, 124, 127, 131, 138, 157, 160, 166, 192, 196, 197, 224, 231, 246, 248, 255, 258, 273, 274, 288
Ikola, Gale William 30
Iliprandi, Giancarlo 216
Imazu, Takao 113
Imura, Fumio 213
Interpub' 152
Ira Advertising 117
Ishii, Masaaki 298
Ito, Katsuichi 122, 156, 292, 304
Iwański, Sławomir 270

J
Jensik, Jerome 212

K
Kakhadze, Kakha 306
KAN 151, 259
Kanchev, Stefan 299
Kannou, Sukeyasu 105
Katsuoka, Shigeo 26, 61, 182, 257
Kishimoto, Kazuo 103
Kogoj, Oskar 275
Koyoda, Fumio 34

Kramer, Burton 11, 16, 35, 119, 148, 184, 217, 223, 238, 239, 300
Krämer, Otto 134
Kündig, Hans 171
Kuwayama, Yasaburo 167, 170, 191, 208

L
Landor Associates 286
Lange, John 291
Laroche, Yvon 268
Larsen, Tim 185
Lawrence, Jonathan 29, 290
LDV United 18
Lienhart, James 66, 90
Logsdon, Chris 40, 271, 289

M
Maes, Frank 210, 293
Mahieu, Johan 24
Malerba, Carlo 85
Martino, Ludovico Antonio 174
MashCreative 36, 186, 189, 226, 249, 252, 295
Masubuchi, Ikuo 89
Matchstic 290
Medina, Fernando 15, 153
Metz, Frederic 81
Meyer, Rudi 14, 282, 284
Miettinen, Esko 149
Milani, Armando 209, 211, 305
Milani, Maurizio 261, 305
Moore, Norman 202
Morfos Diseño 241
Mori, Koji 279
Motter, Othmar 147, 195, 272, 276
Mühlemann, Werner 313
Müller, Jean-Claude 143, 253
Murata, Kazuhiro 180
Murotani, Keizō 244

N
Nagai, Kazumasa 242, 296
Nagai, Yūji 244

Nagata, Katsumi 191
Narimatsu, T. D. 114
Nava, R. 87, 234
Novillo, Cruz 60, 310, 312
Nozaki, Toshinori 168

O
Olyff, Michel 67
Ōtakara, Takuo 108
Otaka, Takeshi 262

P
Parkhurst, Ken 278
Pärtin, Risto 232
Pelletier, Pierre 205
Pirtle, Woody 74

R
Ravan 42, 220
Redstar Design 18
Remington, R. Roger 63, 183
Reyes, Jorge 309
Richez, Jaques 93
Riefenstahl, Peter 99
Rión, Fernando 177
Rosshäusem, B.E. 230
Rousso, Steve 50, 190, 281
Roy, Jacques 163

S
Saito, Soichi 115
Saito, Yoshiharu 33
Saks, Arnold 175
Schockaert, Guy 125
Séguin, Réal 91, 227
Sganzerla, Angelo 236
Śliwka, Karol 263
SocioDesign 207
Soffientini, D. 87, 234
Sotillo, Álvaro 199
Spera, Michele 28
Sprengers, Jozef 165
Stankowski, Anton 155

Stein, Doris 102
Steiner, Henry 128, 251
Studio Artex 111
Studio Meersman 308
Szekeres, István 17

T
Tajima, Kazuo 176
Takata, Masaharu 297
The Studio Temporary 80
Timing, Alliance 46
Today 21, 47, 204
Toida, Hiroshi 145

U
Ubertazzi, A. 87, 234
Ueda, Akisato 144, 302
Ulmer, Peter G. 287
Urban, Dieter 49, 268

V
Van Craesbeeck, Jan 37
Vandek, Jo 129
Vandenbroeke, Bernard 68, 92
van Eerden, Jeroen 137, 139, 188
Vansevenant, Roger 43, 54, 109, 225
Vasco Design 173

W
Walczak, Tytus 58
Witherspoon, Randy Lynn 285
Wunderlich, Sonja 64

Y
Yamamoto, Tatsuhito 193
Yeager, Richard 45

Z
Zahm, Volker 311
Zapf, Hermann 132, 201

ACKNOWLEDGMENTS

This book would not have existed without **Paul Ibou** who allowed me to enter in his world of art and design. He published some wonderful books on logo design such as *Banking Symbols Collection 1 & 2, Animal Symbols 1 & 2, Art Symbols, Logo World* and many others.

As he was so busy, he never found time to finish other book projects that came from his mind. It was thus an absolute honour for me to have the opportunity to collaborate with Paul on this project and hopefully many other future projects as well.

Paul once said to me: "At the age of almost 80, I am at the end of my career. My job is done. The only thing I did not figure out yet, was what would happen with my work, projects and ideas if I wouldn't be here anymore. Now, I know it is safe and will continue to live. To me, you are a godsend.".

Likewise, Paul.

—

I would also like to thank all contributors of this book:

Everyone who submitted their work. I have received more than 600 submissions which were a huge help in making this book possible.

LogoArchive: a study of form language in logo design and a recovery, restoration and archival project by Richard Baird and BP&O. *www.instagram.com/logoarchive*

Canada Modern: a physical and digital archive of Canadian graphic design, with modernism central to its glowing heart. Conceived and produced by Canadian creative director Blair Thomson. *www.canadamodern.org*

My friend Emily Pehar, for helping me unrestrictedly with the translation and correction.

BIBLIOGRAPHY

Ibou, Paul (ed.): *Art Symbols 1;*
Interecho Press, Zandhoven 1992

Ibou, Paul (ed.): *Banking Symbols 1;*
Interecho Press, Zandhoven 1991

Ibou, Paul (ed.): *Banking Symbols 2;*
Interecho Press, Zandhoven 1991

Ibou, Paul: *Logobook - 200 Trademarks and Symbols;* Interecho Press, Zandhoven 1991

Ibou, Paul (ed.): *Logobook 1 - A collection signs and emblems of Flanders - Belgium;*
Interecho Press, Zandhoven 1986

Ibou, Paul (ed.): *Logobook 2 - A collection signs and emblems of Flanders - Belgium;*
Interecho Press, Zandhoven 1987

Ibou, Paul (ed.): *Logobook 3 - A collection signs and emblems of Flanders - Belgium;*
Interecho Press, Zandhoven 1990

Kuwayama, Yasaburo (ed.): *Trademarks & Symbols of the world 1;* Kashiwa Shobo, Tokyo 1987

Kuwayama, Yasaburo (ed.): *Trademarks & Symbols of the world 2;* Kashiwa Shobo, Tokyo 1989

Featured countries
Argentina
Australia
Austria
Belgium
Brazil
Bulgaria
Canada
Colombia
Cuba
Czech Republic
Estonia
Finland
France
Georgia
Germany
Hungary
India
Ireland
Italy
Japan
Luxembourg
Mexico
Poland
Portugal
Russia
Slovenia
Spain
Sweden
Switzerland
The Netherlands
Turkey
Ukraine
United Kingdom
United States of America
Venezuela